Scituate
· C h r o n i c l e s ·

T E D C L A R K E

Charleston · London

THE
History
PRESS

Published by The History Press
Charleston, SC 29403
www.historypress.net

Cover images: Front photo courtesy of Brian Stewart Photography. Back photo courtesy of
the Library of Congress.

First published 2014

Manufactured in the United States

ISBN 978.1.62619.538.7

Library of Congress CIP data applied for.

Contents

A Word from David Ball

It is always good to see new books published about Scituate, a town with an extraordinarily rich and varied history. This newest book will give the reader a great overview of the many events that shaped the town and the individuals who helped steer the town forward.

DAVID BALL
President, Scituate Historical Society

Acknowledgements

I would like to thank the Scituate Historical Society and its president, Dave Ball, for their great help in allowing me to explore their collections and use pictorial materials, as well as for their help in my attempts to get the facts about Scituate as accurate as possible. I was also assisted by the Scituate Public Library and its staff in locating documents and photos.

In any work of this type, many hours are spent doing research and locating images. This involved numerous trips to Scituate, as well as time concentrating on the writing. I wish to thank my wife, Mary Louise Clarke, for her patience and understanding during the completion of this work.

Introduction

S cituate, among the first places to be settled by the Pilgrims branching out from Plymouth, has a fascinating history that stems from those days to the present. Part of it comes from its position on a rocky, ledge-strewn coast, friendly to shipbuilding but not to ships. It is a coast that became famous for its shipwrecks and lighthouses, for the moss gathered from its rocks by Irish immigrants and, most recently (even in the past year), for its valiant fight to withstand ocean storms and the floods that have accompanied them.

Such a place, buoyed by vibrant spirits resistant to the forces of nature, produces extraordinary individuals whose deeds have made their hometown notable, just as they themselves have achieved that status. This book will speak of them, of the town and rocky shores and of the constant conflict between resisting the perils of nature and taking full advantage of its proximity to the sea.

The story of Scituate extends to its practical uses of its resources, even inland, to make the most of its location as a suburb of Boston and a community of the South Shore—uses that have allowed the town to become and remain a desirable place to live both because of and in spite of its coastal location. Its history is one of people who have taken a unique situation and made good use of it.

Like most of the early settlers along the coast of Massachusetts Bay, those who came to Scituate in 1623 or later made good use of what nature had given them, and to a large extent that meant access to the sea. An oft-quoted poem that refers to the settlers at Plymouth speaks about the hardiness of

The landing on a stern and rockbound shore. *Painting* Landing of the Pilgrims, *by Michele Comé, circa 1803–7.*

the people who came to New England and learned to eke out a living on its "stern and rockbound shore" where "the breaking waves dashed high."

The poem referred to the landing of the Pilgrims, who came some years earlier, during which time not much had changed except that most of the best lands along the coast in Plymouth had been taken, and the settlers had begun to explore and then to spread out to nearby places like Scituate, a place where they were joined in goodly numbers by newcomers from Kent in England.

"Scituate" was named for a brook that ran, and still runs, into the harbor: *satuit*, meaning "cold brook" in the language of the Wampanoags who inhabited the area. It seems suitable that the town was named for a water source since it has had such an integral relationship with water both along the coast and in its marshy and pond-strewn interior.

The soil—marshy in places, sandy in others and with plenty of rocks and ledges—was unsuitable for agriculture in the main, so the early settlers turned quickly to fishing and the building of boats. They might have learned such things as planting from a "Squanto" if they'd had one as the Pilgrims did. Such tribes had lived in the area not long before; in fact, John Smith had stopped at the mouth of the North River, charted it and traded with the natives in 1614.

The American Indians who had lived in Scituate just prior to the white settlers' arrival had, like most others of that era, perished in large numbers in the epidemics of European diseases contracted so widely by the natives of the New England coast. Part of the Wampanoag tribe, they had been up to ten thousand in number, but diseases such as smallpox, for which they had no immunity, infected and killed up to 90 percent of many tribes and reduced the numbers of those who lived in and around Scituate to a small number of their previous strength—this during the few years before the Pilgrims dropped anchor in Provincetown and set foot on the sands of Plymouth Harbor. These natives used the rivers for transportation and for food, as can be seen from the fish weirs and mounds of clamshells that have been uncovered.

Even today, the town of Scituate is largely defined by its location—twenty-five miles from Boston, along the rocky coast, but with barrier beaches. It is a place distant from major highways and maintains the look and feel of a small town.

Those who first came to Scituate were soon joined by immigrants from the county of Kent in England. The settlement was governed from Plymouth until incorporated as a town in 1636.

Hanover, Marshfield and Norwell were later carved out from the original town, where fishing was the main industry and still exists today. In the years since then, some interesting lore has come out of Scituate, with its rocky shore, as we'll see in the pages ahead.

Background to Scituate

Location, location, location. In real estate, it's everything. A water view, as we know, has great value; beachfront properties especially are priceless. And towns on the coast of Massachusetts, like Scituate, are among the world's most fortunate holders of water views and waterfront locations. The challenge is to preserve the pristine—to value the views and the brush with the ocean while maintaining a safe distance from its potential perils.

Even if you're a visitor to the Bay State, this great good fortune of oceanfront property is shared to some extent with you because Massachusetts has often shown the civic sensibility to allow everyone the access to most of its views of the Atlantic and even to waterfront and beachfront properties—at least to the low-water line and often the full beach. You can bury your toes in the sands that greet the ocean and feel the surf wash over you no matter where you're from.

Water views can be a spiritual elixir, too, and here's an example: Before I moved to my present location, I could look out the windows and see neighbors' houses, their gardens, streets with a few cars, the sky…and not much else. We moved a mile away, and now I can see the Boston skyline, the harbor, its islands, planes landing at the airport, oceangoing vessels, ferries and, most of all, miles of salt water. Water views make an invigorating difference.

Ocean views, beachfront property and access to the sea itself have brought people to Scituate. The first settlers, of course, approached via the sea and also used the waters for transportation and to earn their livelihood by fishing.

When they built houses, they didn't venture far from the ocean, the first dwellings appearing on Third Cliff, near the harbor on Kent Street, Front Street and, later, along North River or other waterways.

To the early settlers, the proximity of the ocean meant the use of boats for transportation and the availability of fish and shellfish. It meant that they were on the supply lines from England—even the road home, if that's what they chose. To later people, those things mattered less or not at all. Instead, the beaches and the views were important, and they still are.

The coast of Massachusetts was the place where much of the first settlement of New England, and of America, took place. It was not a vacant area, like a new house to be moved into. It had been home to tribes of Native Americans for more than ten thousand years, tribes that had begun as hunting and gathering societies but had evolved into ones that farmed and had developed primitive tools. With these tools, they made things out of leather and ceramics, weaved baskets, made wigwams in which to live and traveled about in canoes. They had traditions, and they valued the waterfront too. Those natives were still here, although in small numbers. They had their sacred places like burying grounds, and they still made their living by hunting and fishing.

In fact, Plymouth Plantation was built where the Pawtuxet tribe had made its home a few years earlier. At that time, only one member of the tribe remained—someone who had been away from home when those diseases came to call. But he would be important to the Pilgrims. His name was Squanto, and he would be a key to the success of the first settlement.

A second man was also key to the early exploration and settlement of Massachusetts: John Smith. The Pilgrims, probably including the first ones to come to Scituate, had read Smith's *Description of New England* and had learned of the area's resources and attractions from reading and following the words of a man who had been there, taken notes and made maps.

Most readers will know Smith from his days in Jamestown, Virginia, but perhaps more importantly, he explored and charted this part of the coast as well, publicizing his findings. There's more to come in the following pages about Squanto and Smith, the two men who were so important in early Massachusetts. It was a smaller world then. To illustrate, for example, Smith and Squanto shared a voyage from Olde England to New England in 1614.

Many colonists, like those who came to Virginia and other colonies on the mid-coast or in the South, came seeking profits, but on the Massachusetts coast, it was often different. Here, families seeking religious freedom were typical. They were often middle-class people, unhappy with religious persecution in England. For example, the Separatists of Plymouth, commonly called the "Pilgrims," had come to America in order to find religious freedom. That was true of the Puritans, too, who came to the northern part of Massachusetts Bay as part of the "Great Migration," as the Puritan exodus to Massachusetts in the 1620s and 1630s was called. It included men like John Winthrop and others who were fleeing King Charles I.

In the early years, the settlers got along well with the natives and often paid for deeds of land they were using that had belonged to the American Indians. (They later learned that those deeds and certain expectations were different in the views of the two peoples.)

Being religious people, nearly every town was built around a church or meetinghouse. In fact, new towns could not be established until they had one. Scituate established its meetinghouse early and had a minister within a few years. Homes would be built close to the church, usually on a village green, while farms and pastures were located on the outskirts. That kind of pattern can still be seen in New England towns. It was a classic New England town plan.

Puritans settled both north and south of Boston, as well as inland along the Charles River, while Separatists (Pilgrims) settled in Plymouth before moving out shortly to places like Duxbury, Scituate and Marshfield, as well as places on Cape Cod.

The patterns of town settlement were much the same, with some differences depending on what ways of life they eventually pursued. These people had left England to establish a colony where they could practice religion in the way they wished, and they meant to form a permanent colony. They had some definite ideas about what an ideal settlement would be like, and having a "clean slate" on which to write, they set out their plan quite clearly.

Winthrop and his followers came on a mission. They believed that the Puritans were God's chosen people and that they must set an example for all who came to America. In order to follow God's will, they believed, one must read the Bible, and it followed that one's children would have to learn to read so that they, too, could read the Bible. Education, then, was important in New England, and schools were set up, including a college in Cambridge that was in time named Harvard College for John Harvard, who had willed his library to the school.

The Separatists who came to Plymouth had strong religious beliefs at the core, but they were also backed financially by "adventurers" whose aim was to make a profit from trading. Among these were people like Timothy

Hatherly and others who were the founders of Scituate. They saw that it was their responsibility to solve problems and plan the future of the colony, and by and large, they were good at that.

Strong religious beliefs were one thing, but these early settlers had to eke out a living on the coast of New England. The way they did that is a hallmark of the early settlers of this area. Since the soil was poor for farming, they soon turned to fishing and later learned to use their own abilities to make things they needed. We call it "Yankee ingenuity."

When America and Britain warred, and manufactured goods were hard to get, Massachusetts, and later other places, built factories and brought the Industrial Revolution to these shores, most notably in Waltham on the Charles River but also on the South Shore in places like Quincy, with its glass manufacturing; Weymouth; Brockton; and other towns with shoemaking. Scituate made ships but didn't have the water power from rivers to become a mill town.

The seaport towns also admitted many immigrants, mostly from Europe. Many of the towns in the area found room for them, including the towns and cities along the coast south of Boston like Scituate, with its large number of Irish immigrants. These newcomers made valuable additions to the labor force. In places like Boston, they were viewed as nuisances. In Scituate, though, they filled a niche that no one else could fill, and they weren't competing with the earlier settlers for jobs and tasks they were filling.

Although it is one of the smallest states, Massachusetts has one of the longest shorelines, 187 miles, most of it along the Atlantic. Glaciation affected the area and left the coast with many inlets—some rocky, some marshy and sandy and most of it lowland. There were several drumlins (sloping, rounded hills left by the glaciers). They make up the many hills along the coast, as well as islands that dot the shoreline. This topography has given Massachusetts Bay its fine harbors, protected inlets and marinas, excellent beaches and splendid vistas. In addition to the geography and topography of the region, there are also stories to go with the scenery and history to go with the geography. These things allow us to put human faces on the stories. It's a curious thing about us human beings—we take more interest when we have people in our stories, for we can relate to them, imagine ourselves in their place and even empathize with them. I'll try to pick some of the most interesting and meaningful people and associate them with particular locations to give readers a fuller view of this wonderful area.

John Smith

THE MAN WHO MADE THE COAST INVITING

When you read stories of the early days in coastal towns, one name emerges more than any other—that of the famed explorer and mapmaker John Smith. And it should, as John Smith did more than any single person to bring traders, fishers and even settlers to both Cape Ann and Cape Cod and, eventually, to the land in between (as well as to the coast of Maine).

Yes, that was the same John Smith who is accurately portrayed as a founder and savior of Jamestown, Virginia, and linked (sometimes to a greater extent than was accurate) with Pocahontas, the Indian princess who did marry an English colonist (but not Smith). His story about Pocahontas and her father Powhatan, the sachem of the tribe, were Smith's own, although none of the individuals involved in the story cast any doubt on it at the time he told it.

But his storytelling could easily have been more colorful while still based on truth. Before his days in Virginia, Smith had fabulous adventures in Europe as a soldier of fortune (most of which are chronicled in *South of Boston*). After Jamestown, he returned to England, but in 1614, he sailed west again and explored the Atlantic coast, including much of the coast of Massachusetts from cape to cape. It was he who named the area "New England." He named many other things as well, as we shall see.

He sailed off the coast of Boston Harbor and looked inland up the mouth of the Charles, which he named for the future Charles I. He was impressed by its width and wrongly believed that it was a major continental river. He and his men also sailed into Cohasset Harbor, where they were assailed by natives who shot arrows at them, driving them off.

He brought fish and pelts back to England. During his attempt to return to New England in 1616, John was captured by French pirates. After a few weeks, Smith escaped from captivity and returned to England. Soon thereafter, he published his expeditions and explorations in *Description of New England*. He started writing accounts of his explorations for the rest of his life. This is where Smith made his major contribution to the settling of the New England coast. He was really an excellent publicist and believed that he could bring people from England to New England by telling the truth and not sugar-coating by saying that people could find gold and riches here.

He told people that they could get rich by working hard because the opportunities came from the soil, the forests, the oceans and the harbors. Fishing, farming, shipbuilding and trading furs and timber were all readily available for those with ambition and the courage to leave their homelands and cross the ocean (a dangerous voyage).

His book also told readers about the climate, flora and fauna of the coastal region from the Penobscot in Maine south to Cape Cod, as well as described the fishing, soils and native tribes. All that was there at the time (the Pilgrims had not yet arrived) was a small number of fishing stations and trading posts used mainly by the French from Canada and the Dutch from New Amsterdam (later New York), for whom furs acquired by the natives were the main currency. Mostly along the Maine coast, ships from Spain, Portugal and Holland took cod and sold them on the other side of the Atlantic.

Although these do not appear to be major enterprises, they showed the visionary Smith the possibilities for future development and the need for English colonists to settle in the New England area before other nations got the same idea. To Smith, New England was a place where English settlers could readily transplant life from their own coastal communities to similar ones in the New World, and he wrote in order to offer guidance and his personal knowledge.

Smith was perhaps the best mapmaker of his time, and some of his maps were of New England. When you draw a map, you have to name the various islands, rivers and capes. Smith did this in large numbers. He had mapped Cape Ann, north of Boston, but he called it "Cape Tragabigzanda." This was a Turkish name, the name of yet another royal princess (Pocahontas was the other) who had "admired" him. He had essentially been her slave, after he, a mercenary soldier, had been taken prisoner during a war. He later escaped to Russia and then found his way home to England.

John Smith. *Engraving, artist unknown, National Portrait Gallery, London.*

When Smith presented his map to Prince Charles, with its many "barbarous" names (the many Native American names), he suggested that Charles should feel free to exchange any of these for "English" ones. Charles went whole-hog and changed lots of them, but even most of his changes have not endured. Only four survive today, one of which is Cape Ann, which Charles named in honor of his mother, Anne (with an *e*), of Denmark. Smith named Massachusetts after the native tribe of that name that he found here, and of course the name remains, as does that of the bay named after it.

There is an interesting spinoff from Smith's single visit to New England that connects him with the other important person from colonial days. One of his lieutenants, Captain Thomas Hunt, engaged in a little enterprise of his own, without Smith's knowledge or approval. He captured some natives and put them aboard a ship bound for Europe. There were twenty Pawtuxets and seven Nausets. Among the captives was the man we know as Squanto. It would not be the first, nor the last, trip across the Atlantic for him.

Squanto

MAN WITHOUT A COUNTRY

Squanto had been captured once before and sold in England to Sir Fernando Gorges, who owned a company that wanted to make money in America. Squanto, who had left behind a family and was a handsome, athletic-looking man, became the consort of an English woman named Lady Jane Smith, with whom he had two children, John and Shandarel. He stayed on the estate of Gorges and was named "Jeremiah Stein." He learned the English language (with an upper-class dialect, no doubt) and became imbued with the culture.

For his part, Gorges was acculturating Squanto to be his representative in America. He wanted to learn more about New England and its people (this was before *Description of New England*). Squanto was a quick learner, had lived along the shore of New England (including Maine), understood about fishing and trading and by now could speak good English.

Squanto stayed in England for nine years, not only learning the English language and culture but also figuring out the motives that led to colonization and trading, motives that would have been foreign to a Native American. Squanto learned what many westerners have *still* not learned: he figured out how capitalism works.

Gorges sent Squanto to New England to serve as an English-speaking guide for his explorers and traders and to interpret for them with the natives along the coast. This was where he met the other seminal figure of New England colonization, John Smith. They appear to have gotten on well.

Smith told Squanto that if he would act as a guide and interpreter, then he would be rewarded by being returned to his people: the Pawtuxets in Plymouth. Squanto sailed with Smith on his 1614 voyage to America. Another ship accompanying them was under the command of Thomas Hunt. When they arrived, Smith set about on his mapping, while Hunt was given the task of trading with the Indians. Squanto was assigned to Hunt, but as we've seen, he instead became one of the twenty-seven natives to be sold into slavery.

These natives were taken to a part of Spain near Gibraltar, but Squanto and some others were rescued by local friar monks, who took them in to teach them Christianity. Squanto became a baptized Catholic and stayed with them until 1618, when he was able to board a ship for Newfoundland. However, he was again captured and this time returned to Gorges—his third eastward crossing. In London, he stayed with a member of the nobility as a horse trainer, learning still more of English ways.

Meanwhile, Hunt's capture of those Indians had turned most of the tribes, and particularly the Nausets, against all white people. Gorges wanted to set things right, so he sent Squanto on still another voyage to try to make peace and improve trade relations. Squanto was told that he could then return to his people. However, in the midst of all those years, disease (probably smallpox) had swept through most of the Indians of the East Coast, including all of Squanto's kinsmen. He was a man without a country, and he was devastated.

Squanto moved to the neighboring village of Nemasket, where he lived among Indians of that area. They had a chief named Massasoit and were part of the Pokanoket tribe. Considering what to do next, Squanto realized that he would be valuable to both the whites and Indians, as Gorges had foreseen, but he could use that value for his own benefit rather than for some trading company. It was 1619. The Pilgrims had not yet come to New Plymouth, Squanto's hometown (named in 1614 by John Smith). Their coming would produce a "perfect storm," a coincidence that even involved their choice of Plymouth as a place for their settlement. In reality, it is likely that both groups chose the spot because of its excellent harbor.

The Pilgrims' first anchorage was at Provincetown, from which they sent a group of men under Myles Standish in exploration. They disturbed an Indian burying ground and stole some buried corn belonging to the Nausets, thus getting off on the wrong foot. During their next expedition, they met and skirmished with natives at what is now called First Encounter Beach in Eastham.

By now, the Pilgrims had decided to look elsewhere and sailed into Plymouth Harbor. It was December, and they had no shelter other than the *Mayflower*, so they lived on board and went ashore each day to erect buildings. In the four months it took to build housing, they saw no one, only wisps of smoke from distant fires. But in March 1621, Samoset, an old fishing companion of Squanto's, walked right into their village and spoke to them in English, no doubt startling them. He told them that he had a friend who spoke even better than he and that Squanto would arrive soon.

It turned out to be six days, and the sachem Massasoit and another man were with Squanto. They negotiated a peace treaty and established trade relations, relying on the skills Squanto had learned in his days in London. Those skills were useful later in negotiations with the governors of Plymouth Colony and with other tribes. He knew practically everyone in Massachusetts and was able to bring them together.

Schoolchildren who may know little about the Pilgrims probably know that Squanto showed them how to use fish to fertilize corn. But he also introduced them to vegetables they had never seen and showed how to tap maple trees for sap and identify which plants could be used as medicine (along with those that were harmful). They also learned to eel and clam and to use marsh grass as insulation.

Although Squanto had shown great kindness and shared useful knowledge with the Pilgrims, he also used his skills to advance his own position, something he had probably learned abroad. Squanto understood, for example, that the natives were afraid of the English for two things: they feared their guns, of course, but they also feared the white man's disease that had wiped out their ancestors. Furthermore, they believed that the English could use disease as a weapon if they chose, but this was based on a lack of scientific information. Squanto knew better but used his knowledge as power.

He increased his status and gained tribute by putting in a good word for someone on the one hand, or by threatening to have the English release the plague against others. He also tried to persuade the Pilgrims that certain Indian tribes were planning an attack on them and attempted to get the Pilgrims to take military action against them. But his tricks were discovered by both sides, and the Indians were particularly outraged, probably because they had thought that he was one of them. Massasoit wanted to get even and pointed to his treaty with the Pilgrims that noted that they must turn over any Indian whom Massasoit wanted to punish. Punishment would have meant death, however, and the Pilgrims needed Squanto, so they delayed

Squanto. *From* The German Kali Works, *1911, sketch.*

turning him over. Massasoit persisted, though, and Governor William Bradford finally agreed to give him up to be executed.

Just as Squanto was to be turned over, an unknown ship appeared on the horizon. It might be a foreign ship—perhaps even an enemy. Squanto's skills as an interpreter might be needed. Bradford was compelled to spare him until the crisis had passed. The threat turned out to be a false one. It was the English ship *Fortune*, bringing badly needed supplies. But the Pilgrims had seen that they needed Squanto—that he was invaluable to them.

Another ship arrived in a short time, bringing new settlers to found a colony in Weymouth that would be called "Wessagusset." That colony would lead to more problems with Indians in that area. Squanto would serve the settlers one more time. Both Plymouth and Weymouth needed food, and Squanto went with them on an expedition to Cape Cod during which he became ill and died. Before his passing, he asked Bradford to pray for him so that he could go to the white man's heaven, perhaps an idea that arose from his days with the monks. The treaty Squanto had negotiated lasted an amazing fifty years, and his early help allowed the Pilgrims to survive through their first winters. Governor Bradford later wrote of Squanto that he was "an instrument sent of God." That treaty was broken when Massasoit died and his son made war on the English settlers, including devastating raids on Scituate.

Moving on from Plymouth

Squanto was the last of the Pawtuxet tribe, whose homeland had been in the area where the Pilgrims settled at Plymouth. There had been about two thousands of them, part of the Wampanoag tribe that lived along the shore, where they took in fish and shellfish. They also cleared the land to raise corn and other vegetables, as well as fruit trees. They used the area for hunting, too.

After the Pilgrims had distributed most of the good coastal land in Plymouth, some of them spread out, over the next two decades, moving north and south. To the south, they moved to Cape Cod, following an old Indian trail (now Route 6A) to found the parts of Sandwich, Barnstable and Yarmouth that were on the Massachusetts Bay side of the Cape. These all became towns by 1639—the only towns on Cape Cod for many years. To the north, they settled from Kingston to Duxbury (famed for its boat- and shipbuilding), Marshfield and Scituate, which had a rocky coast and a good harbor itself.

Myles Standish, William Brewster, John Alden and some others acquired land for farming in Duxbury, but the industry the town became known for started years later—mainly after the Revolution, during which time privateering had decimated the fishing fleets along Massachusetts Bay. Duxbury then began to build ships, and by the end of the 1800s, it had become the largest and most famous shipbuilding town in the world. The wealth that came with that allowed for the construction of grand homes along the bay by the builders. Most renowned were the Westons,

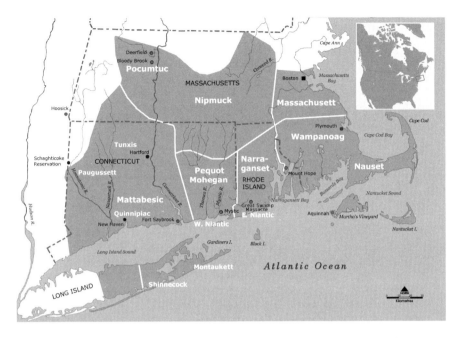

Tribal territories, southern New England. *Photo by Nikater, courtesy of the German Wikipedia.*

whose home, the King Caesar House, is today run as a museum, open to the public.

The era ended with the coming of the clipper ships, which were too large to be built in Duxbury's cramped waterfront space. However, the wealth that had been built along with the ships attracted other wealth in the form of new residents, who came first as summer visitors. When the railroad came to town, they built great houses, and Duxbury became one of the most desirable communities in the state.

Scituate was explored by men from Plymouth who liked the harbor and settled nearby. That was as early as 1623, and the people, who were joined by immigrants from the county of Kent in England, were still governed from Plymouth until incorporated as a town in 1636. In the years since then, some interesting lore has come out of Scituate, with its rocky shore.

Fishing had been a main pursuit of those who came earlier as well. Long before colonists came from England to the shores of Scituate, its beaches and trails were traveled by nomadic natives, a branch of the Wampanoag tribe. Archaeological evidence shows that there were ten thousand or more living here at one time. That was some years before the English settlers came. They were part of an Eastern Woodland Indian culture and were hunters and gatherers who spoke an Algonquian language, as did others of the Wampanoag tribe. This was the northern branch of that tribe.

They were "nomadic" in the sense that Scituate was not their year-round home. It was where they spent spring and summer each year, a practice they held in common with others of their culture, who lived where they could acquire food and moved whenever necessary. In Scituate, their camps were located along the North River and First Herring Brook. They arrived there in the spring when the herring and salmon first began to run. Typically, these natives could be found along waterways or on the coast. This was also the habit of the Massachusetts tribe, which lived just a few miles away in Weymouth and left evidence behind at Great Pond in that town, where a dugout canoe about five hundred years old was found in 1965. Other artifacts were found along other waterways and on the coast.

When summer came, the Indians of Scituate turned to agriculture, planting corn, beans and squash on the barrier island that we now call "Second Cliff," on "Third Cliff" and in the southwestern part of town called now the "Greenfields." The agrarian habits and techniques would have been similar to those that Squanto showed to the Pilgrims just a few years before Scituate was settled. The sandy, rocky soil was really not well suited to farming, but over the years, the natives had developed skills to adapt to these conditions. They were able to raise crops in spite of the limitations. After the harvest moon had shone, most tribes spent the fall and winter seasons inland to the west, some in areas such as the Blue Hills in Quincy and Milton.

With the coming of European fishers and traders in the early seventeenth century, contact was made between whites and "Indians," as they called them. Some of the natives helped the whites with their knowledge of New England fisheries and also traded with them, exchanging furs (for the most part) for manufactured items that the Europeans brought with them. But something else was exchanged—European-generated diseases, primarily smallpox, for which the natives had no immunity.

By 1617, epidemics had spread up and down the coast. These resulted in the deaths of large numbers of natives. Weakened in numbers, and with their regular patterns of life forever altered, it was only a matter of time before they became an underclass in their own land. Of those who survived, some became friendly with the whites and helped them, while a few tribes that had met hostile treatment did not. Under the leadership of the sachem Massasoit, maintaining the terms of a peace agreement engineered by the English-speaking and acculturated Squanto, the groups lived in peace until Massasoit died in 1661. Scituate would play a major role in the hostilities that followed.

Early Settlement of Scituate

In his *History of Scituate, Massachusetts from Its First Settlement to 1831*, Samuel Deane said this about the first settlers: "We are without data as to the first persons who visited Scituate, or the first who took up their residence here. It is certain, however, that the Pilgrims of Plymouth explored the shores very early after their landing, and took notice of the eligible places for settlement…It is certain that William Gillson, Anthony Amiable, Thomas Bird, Nathaniel Tilden, Edward Foster, Henry Rowley, and some others were here before 1628. The above named gentlemen and others, were called 'men of Kent,' having come from that county in England."

The settlers at Plymouth investigated the area around Plymouth for further settlement. Timothy Hatherly arrived at Plymouth in 1623 on the ship *Ann*. Hatherly was one of the adventurers who had financed the Plymouth colony. He had only been in Plymouth a short time before his house burned down with all his possessions, and he returned to England in 1625. However, he sent his niece's husband, Edward Foster, to keep him informed of affairs in Plymouth.

Early settlers seem to have been assigned land in about 1626, although early records are scant. Settlement of Scituate began several years after that of Plymouth, although details differ according to accounts. Some of these say that settlers came to Third Cliff as early as 1623. Timothy Hatherly also gets credit for being the town's first settler.

In 1632, Hatherly returned to Plymouth from England in 1633, expecting to get a grant of land, and he did. The Colony Court ordered that a tract of land be set aside at Satuit that extended from the high-water mark of Satuit Brook three miles into the woods. The tract was granted to James Shirley, John Beauchamp, Richard Andrews and Timothy Hatherly in 1637. Before 1646, Hatherly had bought out the others and had formed a stock company that called itself the "Conihasset Partners." In 1654 and 1656, other grants were added to the original one, and the resulting territory was extended to Hanover and Rockland. These grants were known as the Conihasset Grants.

Hatherly became known as the "Father of Scituate." Later, when there was a large migration to Barnstable and elsewhere, he bought the land of many who wished to leave. In fact, Hatherly often used his personal fortune to benefit the town. Hatherly, easily seen as a hero, continued to spend time and energy on behalf of Plymouth, serving there as an assistant from 1635 to 1658 and meeting regularly with Bradford and the other leaders. He traveled back and forth between Plymouth and Scituate during this time. He was one of those, along with Myles Standish and Edward Winslow, who forged an agreement with Massachusetts Bay Colony for defense when concern arose that there could be trouble with the Indians.

As one of the "Men of Kent," Hatherly showed a different attitude than most of those with whom he had forged that agreement. Many of them, escaping from persecution, were ready to impose that same persecution on those different from themselves. Hatherly and others, like James Cudworth, showed a more liberal attitude in their dealings with the Quakers who came to Scituate and paid for their forbearance with the loss of some of their own rights and political influence. They both regained their standings at last, but their liberal stance probably saved Plymouth Colony (and Scituate) from excesses against the Quakers such as had been shown in Boston with the hanging of Mary Dyer.

The first village was laid out in 1633 along Kent Street. The houses were built of logs, the roofs being thatched. A meetinghouse was also built in 1633 on what is known as Meetinghouse Lane, leading off Kent Street. By the time Reverend John Lothrop arrived in September 1633, nine houses had been built, and that number would grow quickly. This settlement constituted a village about one mile west of the coast and was protected by the cliffs.

The oldest house still standing in town is the Williams-Barker House (now the Barker Tavern). Some believe that it was one of the garrisoned houses since it has windows that look like portholes and seem to fit that purpose. However, this has never been proven.

Scituate was a part of the Plymouth Colony and was first mentioned in print in William Bradford's writings around the year 1634. It should also

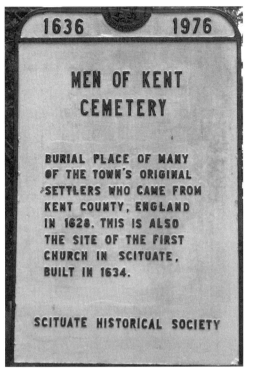

Left: Men of Kent Cemetery. *Photo by author.*

Below: Barker Tavern. *Photo by author.*

be noted that the northern border of Scituate was part of the dividing line between the Plymouth Colony and the Massachusetts Bay Colony.

The village, as planned, ran in a straight line along or off Kent Street. Records show that the first houses built in town were nine palisaded buildings built along Kent Street at the harbor in 1633. Within four years, the number of houses had grown to thirty-one, and by 1636, twenty more had been added. Four garrison houses (fortified as safe places for citizens in the case of an attack) had been built.

The first settlers used the fields left behind by the Indians and planted corn as they had. Those fields had lain fallow for many years since the epidemic, and of course, the glacial soils were not suited for crops, particularly without the kind of improvements the Indians had made that were not known by these new people. But being from coastal England, they *did* know about fishing and shipbuilding, so they used those crafts to supply their food needs and for limited trade, as any seafaring people would do. Satuit Brook, for which the town was named, rose in the hills of the west and wound down through the salt marshes into the tidal waters of the harbor. The name was spelled in various ways.

A secondary settlement took root in North Scituate at Old Country Way and at Old Oaken Bucket Road, and there were also scattered farms in various parts of town. The deed that terminated the old Indian title was signed in 1653 by Josiah Wampatuck and given to Timothy Hatherly. Even today, there are trails in town that are believed to date back to the time of the Indians, especially west of Musquashcut Pond and south of Scituate Harbor.

The peace that had endured under the leadership of Massasoit came to an end under the rule of his son, Metacom, also known as Philip, who reached agreement with other tribes to destroy the English settlements, which he saw as a threat to their land, their way of life and even the existence of the tribes. It had taken the Indians some time to realize that the agreements they had struck with the settlers meant that they gave up the rights to their hunting grounds. For years, in their native tradition, these lands were held in common, but when the settlers began to put up fences as a signal of ownership or construct buildings other than homes, the attitudes of the younger Indians began to sour against the whites. They pressured Metacom to take action.

When war broke out, forces from Plymouth Colony and Massachusetts Bay Colony were allied and under the command of the seventy-year-old James Cudworth of Scituate against Philip/Metacom. Scituate furnished twenty-seven men to this force, more than any other town in Plymouth Colony.

King Philip, or Metacom. *N. Wood, 1911.*

Stockbridge Mill. *Photo by author.*

In the 1675–76 conflict, known as King Philip's War, both sides suffered losses, but in the end, the Indians were vanquished. Scituate suffered from it. In an ambush at Rehoboth, the militia, led by Scituate's Captain Michael Pierce, suffered the loss of fifteen of his townsmen killed, and others died in a raid on Scituate that also resulted in the burning of farms outside of town in May 1676. This was followed by a second raid on the town in which about half the houses in the southern part of town were burned, and several settlers were killed or wounded.

A particular target of the natives was Stockbridge Mill. Apparently, they saw this as a symbol of the changes the Europeans were making to their previous hunting grounds that dramatically altered the landscape—more than a mere homestead or a farm would do. This place suffered severely during King Philip's War. In their attack on the town on May 20, 1676, the military suffered losses, and the number of defenders was low. The Indians first burned the sawmill on Herring Brook, then Captain Joseph Sylvester's house, which stood north of the Episcopal church hill, and then the house of William Blackmore, who was killed the same day.

In their attack on the garrison house, the natives were bravely repulsed. Proceeding in their work, though, they mortally wounded John James and, during the day, reduced as many as nineteen houses and barns to ashes. They were rebuffed, however, in an encounter at the close of the day and driven from the town. A side story took place in the middle of the battle and became a matter of folklore. The Indians, on their way to the garrison house, passed over Walnut Tree Hill near the home of William Cushing and headed toward the house of the Ewells. Mrs. Ewell was alone except for a grandson, John Northey, who was sleeping in a cradle. The house was partially hidden by a hill, and she didn't realize that the tribesmen were headed her way. Alarmed and unthinking, Mrs. Ewell ran out of the house, forgetting to take the child with her in her panic. She reached the garrison, realized that she had left the boy behind, gave the alarm and returned by another route to the house she had left.

Meanwhile, the tribesmen had reached the house but stopped only to remove from the oven the bread she had just put in. Then they rushed to the garrison. The baby was quietly sleeping in the cradle just as she had left it. She carried him safely to the garrison, which had withstood the assault. The Ewells' house was burned, along with others, but the baby had been saved. Mrs. Ewell had a tale to tell for a long time to come.

When the war ended, so did Native American presence in Scituate, for the most part. Nonetheless, despite the outcome, this may be viewed as the most destructive war in New England history, with one out of fifteen able-bodied men killed, crops and villages destroyed and years of bitterness remaining on both sides.

Boundaries

The boundaries of the new town took rather a long while to get straightened out since there was considerable disagreement among abutting towns. The colonial towns seemed intent on granting lands as they were needed and requested by new planters for their farms, fields and residences. Until a settlement would be large enough to become incorporated and able to decide those matters for itself, the colony would make the judgments.

An appeal might come from a lack of suitable farmland, for example, as one did from the Colonial Court records in 1636: "Mr. Hatherly in behalf of the Church at Scituate, complained that the lace was too straite for them, the landes adjacent being Stoney, and not [co]nvenient to plant upon." The court ordered that the people of town "have liberty to seeke out a convenient place for their residing within the Colonie, or that some other lands be layed to them for more comfortable subsistence."

Subsequently, in March 1642, the court set formal borders: "The bounds of Scituate Township, on the westerly side of said Town, shall be up the Indian Head River, to the [P]ond which is the head of said River, and from thence to Accord Pond, and from thence to the Sea, by the line that is the bound between Mass. & Plym." (these last being the Massachusetts Bay and Plymouth Colonies). The ruling settled the town's borders, with one exception: the Indian Head River and its continuation are now the North River.

The line with Hingham (part of which was Cohasset) and Marshfield took longer to settle. Grants were later handed out. One was the "Two-Mile

Grant" along the North River with Marshfield. Rights were granted to both towns to harvest salt hay "two miles along the river and a half a mile from each side." Salt hay doesn't sound like much now, but it was an important part of the diet for farm animals and was also used to insulate houses. The land was ceded back to Marshfield in 1788. The Hatherly Grant of three square miles on the westerly side of the town's court-settled boundaries was part of Scituate and later of Rockland and Abington.

Curiously, the court at Plymouth reserved some of the northern part of Scituate for the exclusive use of certain individuals—Hatherly, Beauchamp and Shirley. It extended from Satuit brook to the Conihasset marshes. Controversies surrounded this grant and took years to adjust. Hatherly didn't wait for all the legalities to be settled. He just stepped up and bought all of it from the others; he divided it into thirty shares, kept one-fourth and sold the rest to a company known as the Conihasset Partners, which functioned as a local government for the area for about two decades.

Disputes with Hingham over the northern border were complicated because Hingham (with its Cohasset section) was part of Massachusetts Bay Colony, while Scituate was part of Plymouth Colony. Here, too, the disagreement was over salt marshes. A committee finally came to an agreement that lasted. The salt marsh meadows were extremely important for many years in Scituate and in other towns where they existed. Their value was such that they were apportioned by towns to the various citizens, and in order to show where their property ended, the owners dug ditches around them. Cedar swamps, too, were split up into lots of eight acres apiece to the settlers, many of whom eventually lived inland.

Later, when inland settlements became the towns of Hanover and Norwell, the new towns were given sections of salt marshes along the estuary. Salt hay was cut by hand or by scythe, while men with long-handled rakes (a foreshadowing of the later Irish mossers) gathered it in so it could be dried on racks and then moved inland by horses, which had to wear special meadow shoes in the muddy grasslands.

Those inland settlements grew fast. At its onset, the town was quite a bit larger than it is presently. The western section, which had added population, became the town of Hanover in 1717; the Two-Mile section went to Marshfield in 1788; and in 1849, South Scituate, which had become a separate town, changed its name to Norwell after a prominent citizen there. Until King Philip's War, most of the settlement had been located near the coast, but it began to spread west along the North River. That's not unique to Scituate nor to Plymouth County. Prominent rivers tended to serve as highways, as they did in the case of the Charles, the Merrimack and the Connecticut. Population and transportation followed these routes, particularly if the river offered water power and fording, though the original impetus was water transportation.

There had also been periods of immigration, some of them due to religious disagreements. In 1640, a contingent moved to Cape Cod and the newly formed town of Barnstable, taking with it nearly half the population. There were also incidents of egress to Barbados, Rehoboth and Swansea. Later groups moved to Norwich, Connecticut; to Newport and Scituate (named after the parent town), Rhode Island; to Chesterfield, Vermont; and to Turner, Harpswell and Topsham, Maine.

Churches

Both custom and law in Massachusetts required the founding or "gathering" of a church in a building or "meetinghouse" before a town could become incorporated. Some later towns actually bought church buildings and brought them in from other places in order to have their petitions accepted for incorporation. In Scituate, the first meetinghouse was built in 1636 on the site of Meetinghouse Lane Cemetery, and the town was incorporated on October 5 of that year.

In order to understand the settlement of New England and the forming of towns such as Scituate, the reader needs a quick-study understanding of what it was that brought the first settlers here. In nearly every case, it was a feeling of religious persecution in England from which they wished to, or in some cases *had* to, escape. The Church of England ruled the roost at that time, and it was extremely restrictive with the way adherents could follow their religion. Dissent was forbidden. Even the slightest deviation—even in the *form* of worship—was harshly punished by imprisonment, banishment or even death. The "heresy" that was happening was hardly harmful to the church. Mostly, the people called Puritans or Separatists wanted to simplify their worship services—we might say to make them less fancy or formal. But even this was too extreme for the bishops of the Church of England, who hunted these dissidents down and administered harsh punishments.

In ways that somehow recall the days of the early Christians in Rome and the Mediterranean, these Puritans had to meet secretly in cells, usually in someone's house or some clandestine place. But that didn't stop the bishop or his inquisitors, who relied on informants to hunt them down and persecute them. Still, it was hard in those days to keep people down when they were seeking freedom. Just then, it was religious freedom, merely the right to do things in their own way without oppression from representatives of the king or the bishops. Later, in America, this type of feeling would arise in regard to self-government and questions about taxing themselves rather than having Parliament or the king impose their wills.

These are things harder to understand in twenty-first century America, where dangers to freedoms seem more remote, but when you think about the chances these people took in seventeenth-century England, you get a glimpse of how much such freedoms meant to them. You also have some insight into the stock from which settlers in Scituate and the rest of New England derive.

The group that came to Scituate can trace its leadership to Reverend John Lothrop, an ordained minister of the Church of England who joined the Independent Church of London, a group that met in Southwark, just across the Thames from London. Members met secretly to avoid the keen eye of Bishop Laud, but they were finally caught and arrested in 1632 and prosecuted for failure to take the oath of loyalty to the established church. Many were jailed in the Clink Prison ("thrown in the Clink"). Lothrop was among those arrested, and when the others were released, he was kept in jail until May 1634. He was then released with the understanding that he would leave for the New World, which he did with many of his followers, coming to Boston on the *Griffin* and then to Scituate within a few days. There they joined with like-minded citizens to form a church that became the First Parish Unitarian Universalist Church of Scituate.

They met in a small log cabin on Meetinghouse Lane, where a monument today commemorates the "Men of Kent" and gravestones of early settlers lie nearby. Over its early decades, however, First Parish went through six ministers and several bouts of dissention, first over the method of baptism and later over a schism involving belief in the Trinity. These weren't simply disagreements. They led to separation of the congregation three different times, as well as the forming of new churches.

The baptism dissent was divisive, and there were other grievances as well, including the lack of good grazing land for cattle. Lothrop petitioned the governor for "a place for the transplanting of us, to the end that God might have more glory and wee [*sic*] more comfort." In 1639, Reverend Lothrop left town, starting a new congregation and town in Barnstable on Cape Cod, with most parishioners following him. The church they built

First Parish Unitarian Universalist Church. *Photo by author.*

there is now part of Sturgis Library, the oldest building in the country housing a public library.

The disagreement over baptism continued through the tenure of Reverend Charles Chauncy, who was said to be an impatient man with stubborn views and the means of expressing them. Chauncy would only perform baptisms by immersion and requested that those who disagreed with him not appear at communion. Some members opposed this and formed a new church in South Scituate, which is now Norwell. The question about the form that baptism would take was not confined to Scituate. It was a matter of heated discussion elsewhere as well. There were other towns whose churches were also divided.

Chauncy was minister until 1654, when he left to become second president of Harvard, exchanging positions with Henry Dunster, the first president, who became the third minister at First Parish. Dunster was then followed by Harvard-trained Nicholas Baker and he by Jeremiah Cushing of Hingham, the first American-born pastor.

The third separation came in the late eighteenth century when half the congregation disagreed with the rest on the subject of the Trinity. But instead of pulling up stakes and moving miles away, those who left only went around the corner to Country Way, where they established the First Trinitarian Church of Scituate in

Henry David Thoreau. *Portrait by Samuel Worcester Rouse.*

1825. It was said that the Trinitarians kept the faith, while the Unitarians kept the furniture.

An outsider who gained fame elsewhere played a small but interesting role in the history of First Parish Church in the nineteenth century. The peripatetic Henry David Thoreau, known chiefly for his writing on philosophic topics, was also a naturalist and a skilled boater, one who often visited the seashore, including Cohasset, Scituate, Duxbury and Cape Cod. His diaries have many references to the sea and even sea serpents, but they also have a reference that ties him to the church under discussion here.

It goes back to 1839, before *Walden, Civil Disobedience* or other essays had made him famous. He met a young woman who had probably written even more than he had—a recent Harvard graduate who was just beginning to keep a diary. Her name was Ellen Devereux Sewell, seventeen, the daughter of the minister of First Parish Church. But he didn't meet her first in Scituate.

Ellen had written perhaps hundreds of letters and kept diaries on a regular basis—diaries that have been kept for posterity and exist today.

They give a good picture of the young woman who came close to marrying Henry David Thoreau in what turned out to be a love triangle gone wrong—as they often do. At Concord, she spent fifteen days with the Thoreau family, and Henry fell hopelessly in love with her, writing in his journal, "There is no remedy for love but to love more."

Henry, however, was not the only young man to feel that way about Ellen Sewell. His older brother, John, had also fallen in love with her. They had both seen Ellen a number of times before, since her aunt and her grandmother had become permanent boarders in the Thoreau house nearly ten years earlier. In fact, she wrote in her diary on July 5, 1832, about an early visit:

> I went to Concord the 26th of June and returned yesterday on the 4th of July; I think that Concord is a very pleasant [place]; I got acquainted with a little girl named Sarah Shattuck, who was 13 years old, and her cousin Elizabeth Shattuck. Edmund and I used to play with Sarah Shattuck every day, and one day we played in her father's little carriage all day long. Elizabeth Shattuck and Sophia Thoreau came to see me one afternoon, and then I went to see Sophia Thoreau the next…
>
> At Concord, yesterday, was independence day and father and Edmund and I went out in the morning and saw two companies of soldiers marching about. In the afternoon, we went out on the common, and coming home we stopped at an Apothecaries and drank some mead. That night, Mr. and Mrs. Simmons, Mr. Chickering, father and mother, and I, all went on the common to hear a band of music, and while we were listening to the music we saw some rockets go up in the sky. The last one that we saw was a very beautiful one.

Seven years later, now a quite beautiful young woman, Ellen couldn't wait to get home and tell her father, a minister, all about her visit to Concord: "Oh, I cannot tell you half I have enjoyed here, till I get home…I have had so many delightful walks with Aunt…and the Mssrs. Thoreau that a full account of them all would fill half a dozen letters."

However, a ripening "friendship" with either of the Thoreau men did not appeal to Reverend Sewell. Even after both brothers proposed to Ellen, he refused to give his consent. He was a straight-line Unitarian, and the Transcendentalism of Emerson and the Thoreau boys was threatening. After Ellen rejected John's proposal, Henry also proposed and was rejected. It was said that Ellen was the only love he would ever have. It is likely that his November 1, 1840 journal entry was related to his lost love:

I thought that the sun of our love should have risen as noiselessly as the sun out of the sea, and we sailors have found ourselves steering between the tropics as if the broad day had lasted forever. You know how the sun comes up from the sea when you stand on the cliff, and doesn't startle you, but everything, and you too are helping it.

Thoreau's daily journal from July 1839 to November 1840 includes many entries related to his feelings of love for Ellen Sewell. Following her father's wishes, Sewell turned down Thoreau's proposal, but a biographer reported that Thoreau carried her memory with him to the end. In 1862, shortly before he died, Thoreau is reported to have said to his sister, Sophia, "I have always loved her."

Reverend Richard Stower was minister of First Parish Church of Scituate from 1992 to 2011. He recently completed a history of the church entitled *A History of the First Parish Church of Scituate, Massachusetts: Its Life and Times.* More than just a chronicle, Stower's book give some interesting glimpses into the church's 380-year history. Stower's stint was a long one, but there have been periods during which the church actually had no minister. His research began in 1998 and took him to England to the British Library and the Southwark Local History Library in London, England. Southwark, of course, was the location of Reverend John Lothrop's congregation, many members of which were persecuted by Bishop Laud and jailed before Lothrop and his followers immigrated to Scituate.

"In 1616, a group of people gathered in Southwark and covenanted together to create an illegal congregation outside the state established Church of England," Stower wrote. Like other such groups, this one left the country. The next twenty-five years became a time known as the Great Migration. Most who left for America were Puritans, but some, like Lothrop and also the Pilgrims, were Separatists.

In addition to Southwark, Stower's research also took him to Kent, where many of the earliest of Scituate's settlers came from, including the first parishioners of the church. Lothrop served in a church there in the town of Egerton early in the seventeenth century.

The church established in Scituate in 1634 is one of the oldest in New England. Several members of the early families of Scituate belonged to the church, such as businessman Thomas Hatherly, along with some boat owners and ship captains. That didn't make it a wealthy organization, and there were periods when it was hard to pay the minister. During the American

Revolution, a barter system was used, and the minister was paid in corn. There were also times when there was no minister, and at other times, the church had to close for lack of heat or funds to pay for it.

Of course, there have also been the divisions due to doctrine or practice. Stover wrote about Reverend Nehemiah Thomas, minister for thirty-nine years, including the time when a split led to the forming of the First Trinitarian Congregational Church around the corner. Stover also wrote of Thomas's successor, Reverend Edmund Sewell, who tried twice to resign because of his health and the epilepsy that plagued him but was refused because he was so beloved by his parishioners. On the other hand, one minister was kicked out of the Satuit Lodge of Masons for refusing to pay dues. He left the ministry later, became a gold miner and married a feminist attorney. Of course, there was the love triangle between the Thoreau brothers and Ellen Sewell, daughter of the minister. During the Civil War, women from the church made bandages for Union soldiers, and after the war, they raised money by selling blankets and other things so they could help a school in South Carolina educate the children of former slaves.

Stover also wrote about the six buildings that have housed the church over the years. The first three were on Meetinghouse Lane, and the fourth was on Lawson Common. The fifth building burned down on the Fourth of July in 1879 when some boys got careless with firecrackers. The current building is on First Parish Road, built in 1881. In 1938, the weathervane was blown off during a great hurricane, and twenty-five years later, a helicopter was used in an attempt to repair the steeple.

Stover said, "One of the reasons I wanted to write the book was to raise the historical visibility of Scituate because it played an important part in the religious history of our nation. I believe that the democratic governance of the colonial congregations laid the groundwork for our civil democracy. The controversies over the manner of baptism led to the growing diversity of theological perspectives leading to the religious freedom and pluralism that we enjoy today."

Geography

In most cases, the history of a place depends a great deal on its geography, and that's certainly true of Scituate. That "location" we spoke of ties in here particularly. It is located on the Atlantic coast, 25.0 miles southeast of Boston, so it's within the metropolitan area. It's bordered by Cohasset to the north; Marshfield to the south; and Hanover, Hingham and Norwell to the west. It's one of the communities known collectively as the South Shore. Of its 31.6 square miles, just over half is land; the rest is water.

The section of Scituate called Humarock was once connected to the rest of town but can now only be reached through Marshfield. In 1898, the fierce Portland Gale washed out the connection and moved the mouth of the South River, shifting it northward. The terrain of the town is not uniform. In the south, there are salt marshes along the North River. But it is sandy around Scituate Harbor (in the middle), and in the north at Minot there are some exposed granite ledges, including the one on which the famous lighthouse stands. The inland area has stands of woods, as well as brooks and rivers, including Satuit Brook.

For many years, access to the ocean was Scituate's only major means of transportation. It has no freeway. The major road through the South Shore is Route 3, which runs from Braintree to Cape Cod, traveling through neighboring Norwell, but at a distance from Scituate. Even today, the town's major highway is Route 3A, a rather narrow highway. Connecting that and Route 3 is Route 123, another state road that runs a few miles through town to the west through Norwell after its junction with 3A. In its Scituate section, that road is known as Chief Justice Cushing Highway (named for Chief Justice William Cushing, who lived in the town).

The railroad is relatively recent. It began in town in the middle of the nineteenth century, was discontinued in 1959 and resumed in 2007 with the institution of the T's Greenbush Line, which parallels 3A and has stops in Greenbush (the terminus) and North Scituate. The line connects to Boston through Braintree. Scituate has no airport, although neighboring Marshfield does.

Its Atlantic coast is Scituate's chief geographic feature and the one most associated with it. It is nearly eight miles long, with Scituate Harbor located at about its midpoint. With ten feet of water, the harbor is partially enclosed, with Cedar Point and the Scituate Lighthouse to the northeast and Crow Point on the southeast at First Cliff. The harbor, which attracted settlers from Plymouth in the first place, remains an important resource, particularly for recreation. Boats of all sorts fill it, particularly in the summer—fishing boats, sailboats, motorboats—as many as 1,200 recreational boats during the season. The town runs a marina with slips for 200 boats.

The coast also has four high cliffs that serve to protect the shore, but they also are subject to erosion and changes in shape. Three of these are north of the mouth of the North River, while Fourth Cliff was separated from the islands by the Portland Gale of 1898 and lies to the south as an island, essentially, along with Humarock and Rexhame Beach.

The three Massachusetts towns of Scituate, Marshfield and Duxbury are particularly susceptible to the dangers of storm surges, coastal erosion and sea-level rise. In fact, Jim O'Connell believes that Scituate is the most vulnerable coastal community in the state. He should know. Besides being a coastal geologist and coastal land-use specialist, O'Connell lives in the seaside village of Brant Rock, just south of Scituate. "Scituate is the most hazardous community in Massachusetts when it comes to damage done by erosion and storms," he noted.

When the glaciers retreated north about ten to fifteen thousand years ago, the North and South Rivers served as channels for the melt water. The North River, at the *southern* border of the town, is a tidal river twelve miles in length that begins where Herring Brook joins the Indian Head River. At that point, it separates Norwell and Pembroke. Little Bridge on Route 3A crosses the river from Scituate into Norwell. The river forms the border between those towns for three miles as it flows south into Massachusetts Bay at New Inlet, where it also joins the mouth of the South River as it flows north. It was named a "scenic river" in 1979 by the Commonwealth of Massachusetts

Bathing on a Scituate beach near Glenwood Cottage, circa 1890. *Scituate Historical Society.*

and is protected by the North River Commission. The construction of housing in towns upriver and along the tributaries of the river has led to pollution that often required the closing of shellfish beds. Although narrow in many places, the North River is deep and winding. Its history is one of shipbuilding in its early days, while more recently, it has become a wildlife sanctuary and is enjoyed for its fishing and boating, especially with kayaks. Another source of recreation in Scituate is its shore.

The town has some fine beaches, covered mainly with sand or smooth pebbles. Minot, Egypt, Sand Hills and Peggotty are the main ones, but there are many others. Summer visitors often rent cottages on Humarock Beach as well. Parking at beaches is limited, especially for nonresidents. Peggotty has an interesting name, as it was actually named for a character in a Dickens novel, *David Copperfield.*

The town also has elevated barrier beaches. These protect the shore from ocean storms but are delicate and valuable ecosystems. Those in Scituate add beauty to the seascape. The Humarock/Rexhame Beach, accessible through Marshfield, is the sixteenth-largest such landform in the state. The shoreline in Scituate may be considered its most valuable resource, and it is sensitive to nature but also to increased development. Its fine harbor is haven to many recreational boats. It, too, can be subject to intense use and requires protection.

Scituate has many streams and extensive wetlands. Poor drainage has been and still is an issue in some areas, complicated by a demand for building new homes. Overdevelopment is a potential problem. Most of the town's drinking water comes from six public wells and the rest from the reservoir. The First Herring Brook watershed has three of the wells. This area is a product of the glacial period, when glacial till was left on top of the bedrock in much of Scituate's uplands. The brook is confined by salt marsh and sediments to an area upstream of its juncture with the North River.

Such a place, buoyed by vibrant spirits resistant to the forces of nature, produces extraordinary individuals whose deeds have made their hometown notable. This book will speak of some of them, of the town and rocky shores and of the constant conflict between resisting the perils of nature and taking full advantage of its proximity to the sea. The story of Scituate extends to the practical uses of its resources, even inland, to make the most of its location as a suburb of Boston and community of the South Shore—uses that have allowed the town to become and remain a desirable place to live both because of and in spite of its coastal location. Its history is one of people who have taken a unique situation and made good use of it.

"The Spit" is a land area in the mouth of the North River and at the southern edge of Third Cliff. A small barrier island washed by tides, it is a major regional recreation area for residents and boaters. Local residents reach it by disembarking from a public boat launching area in Scituate (Driftway Park) or from several private local boat launching areas, as well as from other points on the South Shore. It is the site of a nesting area for the endangered piping plover and the threatened least tern. The area along the Driftway has become a regional recreational resource for golfers and boaters.

A large land area, formerly owned by the Boston Sand & Gravel Company, was acquired by the town in the 1970s. Through efforts of many dedicated residents, there are now numerous recreational and open space resources in this area, including a public golf course (Widow's Walk); a private golf course (Scituate Country Club); a fishing pier; a trail system available to the public, including a newly constructed active bike trail along the Driftway; an informal playing field; a boat launching ramp; and a viewing area with picnic tables and grills.

Fishing

When the "Men of Kent" arrived in Scituate, they had no skills as farmers or fishermen as many of those who settled on the North Shore had. They were, however, an exceptional group of learned gentlemen, some college educated, and from the upper classes. But in order to eat— indeed, in order to survive—they had to learn to get food from the ground or from the sea, so they had to learn farming, fishing and even shipbuilding. It was obvious to these intelligent men that the yield from the sea would surpass that from the land, particularly since the soil was nonproductive, and so the sea was where they cast their oars primarily. They also used their boats for coastal trading in the summer months.

Beginning with these early settlers, the shore has always been the focus of life in Scituate, and a fishing station was established as early as 1633. Everybody fished. In his *Description of New England*, John Smith said so, claiming that any child of twelve, boy or girl, could fish and even spin (make) the line with which to catch fish. Men of Scituate sent to England for cod hooks and lines, mackerel hooks and lines, herring nets and seines, shark hooks, bass nets, squid lines and eel pots. Soon they set to work with the initiative for which New Englanders were to become famous, and they established a trade that made them much money. Laws were made to protect the fisheries, and exemptions were made for fishermen from things like military service.

Fishing and shipbuilding had come to the North Shore of Massachusetts Bay with fishermen who emigrated from coastal Devon, England, or from the

Channel Islands—parts of England where fishermen had been sailing farther from home in order to find more plentiful supplies of fish. They had fished off Nova Scotia and Newfoundland before coming to New England waters. Here they found fish on Stellwagen Banks and off the coast of Cape Ann. Cod were taken there, and over time New England fishermen learned which places were the best places to fish and how to build boats that would get them quickly to the fishing areas as well as boats that would be easy to handle in the choppy waters. They also learned to dry and salt the fish on flakes in order to preserve them for whatever voyages lay ahead. Often they shipped their catches to warm climates like the West Indies, where they sold them, providing an inexpensive, protein-rich food for the slaves working on plantations.

The fish to be found in and around Scituate Harbor were not the cod taken so plentifully off Cape Ann. They were usually mackerel, and at first they were caught over the sides of small boats. The fishing industry grew, however, as did the building of boats and ships. By the end of the seventeenth century and midway through the next, these were thriving. So was the harvesting and sale of salt hay, which could be sold or bartered since it was a commodity that was not found in many other places. Farming continued but never became a major industry. The "Men of Kent" were quick to realize this and became skilled at making practical use of those things available to them.

Fishing, naturally, required proper vessels. At first, that meant following the examples of North Shore communities like Marblehead and Gloucester, whose residents had designed boats such as shallops and schooners meant for fishing. Marblehead schooners were suitable for Scituate Harbor, too, where a commercial fishing industry began to take root later than one on the North Shore, about in the year 1700. The shallops they fished from were open boats (like the one moored in Plymouth Harbor near the *Mayflower*). These evolved over time into two-masters with covered decks that were fairly fast.

The mackerel ran from spring to fall in very large schools. Prior to the Revolution, the fleet of fishing boats had reached thirty vessels, some gathering one thousand barrels of fish in a single season. Mackerel were not dried as cod were. Instead, they was packed in barrels with brine. At that time, Noah Nash built barrels at his cooperage at Scituate Harbor out of oak and ash trees cut locally. Fish, as well as local lumber, were traded in the West Indies and brought sugar, molasses and tapioca, while the southern plantations provided rice, flour made from wheat, tobacco and indigo. The fishing vessels were converted for this use during the summer months, but this trading was hazardous. Ruth Vinal Jenkins, who lived at the harbor, lost two husbands and a son at sea. While the fishing industry persisted, it was interrupted twice by British blockades during the Revolution and especially during the War of 1812. The number of vessels began to diminish, and by the time of Civil War and the abolition of slavery, the trading of fish to the West Indies and the South had ended. The availability of mackerel varied, too, as Deane wrote:

> Our vessels now find them less abundant, and farther from their former haunts. They used to set into the bay early in May, and again in autumn: but now they are found at Block Island channel in May—at George's Bank and Nantucket shoals in the summer, and at Mount [D]esert and along the shores of Maine in the autumn. Those first taken are lean, and favor the commonly received opinion, that they lie, in the muddy bottom, in the winter: but towards the winter they are found well fed, fat and delicious. The full grown mackerel vary in weight from one to two and three pounds. The fattest, taken in the autumn, are not generally of the largest size.

Fishermen in Scituate now take cod, but this change in the availability of fish is echoed in a current paucity of codfish and an attempt to use scientific means to correct the unevenness in the supply. After four hundred years of catching codfish, overfishing has led the government to restrict large-scale fishing and to close some fishing areas off the Massachusetts coast. According to Frank Mirarchi, a retired commercial fisherman from Scituate, "In 2009, four months out of the year were closed [to fishing]. We had, I think, thirty days a year we could fish, and we could only catch eight hundred pounds a day…It was very, very difficult, and there's no enthusiasm to go back to that level."

In 2010, the government began to lift those restrictions on fishing for large clusters of cod that had been coming to the area each winter to spawn. But that allowed things to go to the opposite extreme, where fishermen began to catch cod before they were able to reproduce; this led to a *reduction* in the cod population in the area.

"We need to find a happy medium where we're balancing our ability to earn a living catching fish and the need of cod to be by themselves for a while to reproduce," Mirarchi said. Now a grant of $150,000 for a research project was approved in Scituate whereby research will be conducted on the spawning behavior of cod. Researchers and fishermen will work together to catch about 150 spawning cod, implant electronic tags in them and release them back into the ocean. By tracking the fish, scientists hope to learn where fish are spawning.

Atlantic codfish. *Photo by Hans-Petter Fjeld.*

"It's like E-ZPass," explained Chris McGuire, a marine program director "The tags that are inserted in fish are like the things you have on your windshield. We put thirty-eight receivers under water. Any time a tagged fish swims in range of a receiver, it records that information." When spawning areas are identified, small-scale closings can be put into effect to allow the fish to procreate. Although that will limit fishermen to some extent, many of those from Scituate favor it so that the long-term survival of the fish can be ensured.

Meanwhile, a lively shipbuilding industry had begun by then on the North River, both in support of the fishing industry and as a commercial enterprise that furnished ships for Boston, Salem and other ports. From the harbor, there was also regular packet service to Boston.

Shipbuilding

The first builder of ships at the harbor was Will James, who began in about the year 1646, when he dug a dock from which his ships were launched. However, it was North River that became known for shipbuilding well beyond the South Shore. Wherever there was firm ground on either side of the river—at nearly every bend—there was a shipyard humming with activity or a landing for boats. The vessels built along the river were floated downstream on high tide or on several high tides, and the finishing touches took place in Marshfield near the mouth of the South River. Jesse Dunbar and then Job Otis are credited with beginning the craft at their location, but the building of ships soon became prominent along the length of the river. North River shipyards built some ships that became well known in American history, as well as many lesser-known vessels, for which there was a great demand.

Some of these were the great whalers built for New Bedford and Nantucket for the half century or more when those were the great whaling ports. These were vessels of greater than three hundred tons, but the largest ship known to have been launched from North River yards was a merchantman built in 1812 by William Delano, an ancestor of Franklin Delano Roosevelt. It was nearly five hundred tons.

In the early years, Scituate had fine stands of timber inland from the coast. Trees from these forests became spars and masts of ships built along the river. For a time, it was feared that this supply was running thin. Elisha Foster said that his friends tried to dissuade him from becoming a shipwright for this reason, but he kept on running his business successfully until 1800, and his sons after him. Like Foster, builders were able to keep up with production without diminishing the number of trees to any damaging extent.

Not only were many ships built in this locale, but many shipwrights also learned their craft on the banks of the North River and took those skills with them elsewhere up and down the coast. It could easily be said that a person could visit shipyards and navy yards along the whole coast and meet craftsmen from Scituate or the North River who had also worked or were educated there.

The shipbuilding industry on the North River produced more than 1,025 ships between 1650 and 1870. At each suitable spot along the river, there was either a shipyard or a landing. The vessels were built in the yards, floated downstream over a period of several flood tides and outfitted for sea in Marshfield near the mouth of the South River.

Like most major rivers, the North acted like a highway along which settlements sprouted. Shipbuilding became important to those settlements, including (and most importantly) Scituate. Those skilled craftsmen built watercraft for whaling and fishing ports, as well as trading centers like Boston and Salem. From its inception as a shipbuilding center in the 1600s and for more than two hundred years, more than one thousand vessels were built on the North River, most of them significant or sizable ships.

The industry reached its peak between 1799 and 1804, when 115 vessels were launched. After that, the supply of local white oak and white pine began to diminish, and a sandbar at the mouth of the river limited the size of the craft that could be built. As ship tonnage increased, the deeper ports of Boston, New York and Bath, Maine, became the centers of shipbuilding; most of the North River's shipwrights moved to these locations. The last ship to be launched on the North River, the *Helen M. Foster*, slid down the ways at Chittenden's yard in Norwell in June 1871. The former shipyards are marked today only by placards erected in 1919 by the North River Historical Association.

The best-known ship built along this river was the *Columbia*, built at Hobart's Landing on the Scituate side of the river by James Briggs, a prominent shipwright. His yard was just upstream from Doggett's Ferry (now Little Bridge). Briggs had a fair amount of fame locally in his own right, even without the famous ship that was to circumnavigate the globe.

At the time of the Revolution, the soldiers had to furnish their own muskets, but James Briggs had none. Undaunted, he reported for duty with a stick over his shoulder. When his superior officer asked him what he intended to do, James Briggs cheerfully replied that he was going to knock down the first British soldier he met and take away his musket. History does not record whether he actually carried this out, but we do know that when James Briggs returned to Scituate, he was carrying a British musket.

Following the Revolution and with the formation of the new country, visionaries looked to the west, particularly to the opposite coast, where they learned about the Oregon Territory where both America and Great Britain had competing interests. There would be a race to stake claims to it by exploration and settlement. A group from the Massachusetts Bay area that included Boston architect Charles Bulfinch, as well as one of the Salem Derbys and Captain Crowell Hatch of Cambridge, was willing to stake $50,000 in a voyage to the unknown Northwest.

This group bought two ships for the expedition, one of them definitely built on the North River, the second probably built there. *Columbia* was built in 1773 at Hobart's Landing; it was a relatively small ship of two hundred tons and eighty-three feet in length. It would be captained by John Kendrick of Wareham. The *Lady Washington* was smaller. It was captained by Robert Gray. The plan was to trade with the Indians for furs and then sail on to China, trade the furs for tea and bring that back to Boston. They filled the ships with hardware, beads and other manufactured items to trade for furs.

The trip was long and arduous—around Cape Horn and up the Pacific coast to Oregon. They had trouble with scurvy, with Indians and with collecting the furs in a timely way; they also met ships from both Spain and Britain that were on similar missions.

We also know that the two captains changed ships at some point, whether in Oregon or later, and that the *Columbia* stopped at Hawaii, where a native prince named Attoo joined them. At Canton, China, after exchanging furs for tea, Captain Gray took the *Columbia* south around Africa and on to Boston, the first American ship to sail around the globe. After a three-year voyage, they were met by great excitement and celebration. The governor, John Hancock, gave a dinner for the owners and officers of the *Columbia*, and the Hawaiian prince, Attoo, made a striking statement in his gorgeous yellow and scarlet-feathered cloak (since sent to the Museum of Fine Arts).

On his second trip to Oregon, Captain Gray discovered the large river that he named for his ship *Columbia*, which was built in Scituate by James Briggs and on which he had traveled so far. The trips helped to establish trade relations in the Northwest and staked a claim for American ownership of the territory.

Another famous North River ship was *Grand Turk*, bought by Elias Haskett Derby of Salem and paid for mostly by scarce rum and butter. As a privateer during the Revolution, it captured sixteen British ships, making

The *Columbia. Replica at Disneyland, SolarSurfer.*

a fine profit. It also sailed to China after the war, the first New England vessel to do so.

A customer brought a North River connection to another significant event in American history. It came about at the Brick Kiln Yard on the river. The customer was William Rotch of Nantucket, a Quaker who had the *Beaver* built for him there. It was subsequently sailed from London in 1773 with a cargo of tea for Boston. That cargo, along with the cargoes of the *Dartmouth* and *Eleanor* (also owned by Rotch), were prevented from unloading by the Patriots, led by Sam Adams. A mass meeting was held at the Old South Meetinghouse that led to a disturbance known as the "Boston Tea Party," during which the cargo of tea was systematically dumped overboard into Boston Harbor. Today, a replica of the *Beaver* is part of the display at the Boson Tea Party Museum on Fort Point Channel. The original ship, relieved of its tea, resumed its usual role in the whaling industry.

Another Rotch vessel from the Brick Kiln Yard was the *Bedford*, the first American ship to visit London after the Revolution bearing the American flag. It also bore a cargo of whale oil. Still another whaler built for Rotch, the *Maria*, lasted ninety years in service, mostly as a whaler, and was known to be very fast.

The Quakers (Society of Friends) left England for religious reasons at about the same time as the Puritans. They were not welcomed, however, in most communities. Still, some people in Scituate were more open to them, and the Quakers established a group with a meetinghouse near Greenbush. One of them was Edward Wanton (a former officer of the King's Guard in Boston), who moved to the town with his family. He began building ships around the year 1660 and was joined by his sons in that enterprise. Although the sons, too, were Quakers, both took part in privateering off the coast of Newport. One of them married a Congregationalist, despite the objections of both churches, and later became governor of Rhode Island for two terms.

Another famous name appears in the annals of shipbuilders along North River. Benjamin Delano, a descendant of Philip de la Noye and ancestor of Franklin Delano Roosevelt, came to America in 1621 on the *Fortune* and was the first of his family to live in Scituate. The family descended from French Huguenot stock, French Protestants who had befriended the Pilgrims while they were in Leyden (Holland). One branch of the family settled in Fairhaven, and FDR was a descendant.

Benjamin's son, William, built ships in the Wanton yard, too. He built the two largest ships made on the North River. He also built the only three-storied house on the North River and married Sarah Hart, whose father was master builder of the USS *Constitution*. The anchors for "Old Ironsides" were forged at Luddam's Ford, where Clapp Rubber Works later stood.

The two large vessels built by William Delano were the *Mt. Vernon* and the very fast whaler *Lady Madison*. The former made the westward voyage across the Atlantic in only eighteen days, a record that stood for seven years. The ship was owned by Thomas Hazard and his son-in-law, Jacob Barker, a Quaker and a friend of James Madison who had friends in the nation's capital. The other vessel was the *Lady Madison*. According to a story, the ship was well overdue on a voyage and had no insurance on it. Barker went to an agent, explained what was happening and asked the agent to draw up a policy but not to sign it for a few days. Within a few days, Barker learned that his ship had been lost, so he went back to the agent and told him, "If thee has not signed the policy, thee need not do so as I have heard from my ship." The agent thought that he meant that the ship was safe, so in order to collect the premium, he told Barker that he had already signed. Barker paid the premium and took the policy, telling the agent that he had indeed heard from his ship and that it had foundered. The two men settled for half the insurance. Benjamin's brother, Edward Hart Delano, worked in a number of shipyards and built the flagship of Admiral Farragut, victor at the Battle of Mobile Bay in the Civil War.

After the Wantons had all left, the shipyard was owned by Elisha Foster and his sons. They built the *Smyrna* for the famed Ezra Weston of Duxbury, who was himself a premier shipbuilder. It had to be an outstanding ship to handle since it traveled to Odessa (Russia) on the Black Sea, requiring it to pass through the Bosphorus, famed in Greek mythology for the danger it posed to ships. The American ship crossed through in 1850 against strong, steady winds and an adverse current. On its way back, weeks later, it met ships that had tried and failed to make the same passage. *Smyrna* made the trip in a record forty-two days. The Fosters also built the whaler *Pagoda*, which earned a fortune for its owners over the course of sixty-four years, obviously a well-made ship. That ship was mentioned in Richard Henry Dana's *Two Years Before the Mast* and had a captain's cabin with a berth that remained level no matter how the ship rolled, as well as an overhead compass that showed the skipper while he lay in his berth whether it was on course.

For 351 years, people along the North River from its mouth on the Atlantic and eight miles inland to what was the village of Hanover lived in an environment of shipbuilding. Those who lived in the area could hear the pounding of hammers on anvils and saws cutting through wood as more than 1,025 ships were built and slid down the ways in more than twenty shipyards. The last, the schooner *Helen M. Foster*, closed that chapter of life in Scituate and its environs as the "River of a Thousand Ships," ships that made the North River famous around the world. Shipbuilding in Scituate and along the North River stayed the course for a long time and makes up a significant part of the history and heritage of the town.

Historian C. Wellington Furlong wrote an essay that, in part, mentions a trip to Oregon, where he reflected on the impact of people from Scituate on that area. You can read it on the Scituate Historical Society's website. Following is a summary of what he wrote.

One place he visited was the state capital in Salem, Oregon, which had murals in its foyer depicting an exchange of trade goods on the Columbia River, where a band of natives were trading with Captain Robert Gray of Boston. Furlong noted that most of Gray's crew were descendants of the "Men of Kent," where Gray's great-grandfather had settled in 1643. The murals also show the *Columbia*, whose sailors discovered the great river named for it.

Touching on the other great resonance of the voyages of *Columbia*, Furlong recalled that President Thomas Jefferson, having read Gray's report on the discovery of the Columbia River, was convinced that it was the legendary "River of the West," with headwaters near those of the Missouri, and considered the possibility of creating an inland water route from the Mississippi to the Pacific Ocean. This led to his sending Lewis and Clark on their expedition of exploration.

Furlong also recalled how many from New England followed the Oregon Trail, that many locations in that state are named for ones in this part of the country and that older Indians called all whites "Boston men." He also added to the notions attached to the term "Yankee" trader by relating how Gray, in one case, was able to get the natives to trade two hundred otter skins for a single chisel. He meant the tool, of course, but the word does have another meaning.

After the decline of the shipbuilding industry, the rivers became the sites of pleasure boating activities. The North River Boat Club was formed in 1893, and its clubhouse was built just to the east of the Union Street Bridge. In 1894, the first power launch arrived on the rivers. The area had become increasingly popular as a summer resort since the 1880s, and summer folk were to have a strong influence on the river. In 1885, a bridge was built to Humarock to accommodate the resort hotel. Later, upstream, power boaters persuaded the railroad to raise its bridge and convinced the state to remove the rocks from the stretch of river just west of the Union Street Bridge known as "Rocky Reach."

The Irish Riviera

Irish eyes are smiling in Scituate—about half the eyes in town anyway. According to a 2011 report, Scituate is the most Irish town in America, with 47.5 percent of the people in town being of Irish descent based on the U.S. Census. That number is easily the largest percentage in America. It's probably not surprising that sixteen communities on the South Shore have the highest percentages of Irish living in them. Fewer than Scituate but still with more than 44 percent Irish are Braintree, Hull, Marshfield, Avon, Pembroke and Milton. In fact, the South Shore, and particularly Scituate, is often called the "Irish Riviera." That name is often applied to Scituate, but it can also mean neighboring communities as well, or even the whole South Shore. Irish Americans are the dominant ethnic group in suburban Boston, but even more so south of the city, a trend that has held for decades.

Massachusetts isn't the only state with an Irish Riviera. The name has also been used for Irish enclaves on the New Jersey shore and for Rockaway in Queens, New York. As might be expected, these places are near water.

Scituate has been called the Irish Riviera since at least the 1930s. Dave Ball, president of the Scituate Historical Society, noted that he doesn't hear the phrase used as much as before. "Twenty years ago, you certainly did. I don't know why that is—I don't think anything changed dramatically," he said. Ball taught sixth grade in Scituate for many years, and he said that whenever he asked how many of his students were of Irish descent, "90 percent put their hands up. Open a phonebook in the town, and you'll find Irish surnames like Sweeney, O'Neil, Curran."

According to Thomas O'Connor, historian at Boston College and author of several books, including *The Boston Irish: A Political History*, "Irish with a great deal of money or a great deal of political clout began to move out and down into the South Shore. You could see them buy large houses on spits of land near the ocean in Marshfield, Scituate, and Cohasset—all the way down to Hyannis."

Irish families began to come to the South Shore in large numbers after World War II, although Scituate had a head start on that migration. Many of the families came from sections of Boston when they began to move up economically. After the war, as servicemen returned home, they often married and began to raise families, so they needed houses and wanted backyards and a little greenery.

They might not have been able to get a mortgage in Boston, but they could qualify in suburban areas, where prices were cheaper. This was not likely to be western suburbs like Newton or Wellesley nor northern ones like Swampscott and Marblehead—all too pricey. Plus many Boston residents were more oriented to the south of Boston rather than other directions. Moving south made sense—to Quincy, Weymouth, Braintree, Milton and especially to Scituate, where there was already an Irish nucleus. That was particularly true of people living in South Boston, Dorchester and Hyde Park, who did much of the moving. They were used to visiting beaches on the South Shore like Wollaston, Hough's Neck or Nantasket. That nucleus was formed by the generations of Irish families who came to the town for its thriving Irish mossing industry, which was established in the mid-1800s by an Irish immigrant, Daniel Ward.

In 1790, Reverend John Thayer became the first Catholic priest to visit Scituate. Thayer was a converted minister and the first priest to be ordained in all of New England. Not long afterward, in 1798, Father John Cheverus visited Plymouth and stopped at Scituate on the way back to Boston. He would become Bishop John Cheverus in 1810, the first bishop of Boston. While in Scituate, Father Cheverus performed a baptism, according to his records. "He baptized in the family of one Michael Clapp, the only Catholic family in town." Cheverus visited Catholic families on the South Shore, bringing instruction books so they could practice their religion at home since they had no churches at that time. In order to go to mass or receive the sacraments, they would have to go to Boston.

A large number of Irish Catholics would be coming to Scituate, however, in the years ahead. The first of them would come for the fishing possibilities, just as fishermen from other parts of the British Isles and elsewhere had visited New England and just as the "Men of Kent" had come to Scituate from Plymouth and from Kent to take up fishing early in their settlement. Those fish, sold elsewhere, helped to establish Scituate's reputation as a good fishing area.

Two Irish fishermen who came to Scituate in 1847 were Daniel Ward and Miles O'Brien. Ward, in particular, would make his presence known, both as a man of the sea and as a religious person. Ward settled on Third Cliff with his three sons and his partner, O'Brien. They fished at first but were surprised to see a familiar moss on the rocks near the shore. They recognized it as the same plant that grew on the shores of their native Ireland. The moss was a species known as carrageen or "Irish moss." They quickly realized that here was a product they could harvest and sell—an industry they knew well and could do better at than they could with fishing. It had sold well in Ireland as an emulsifier and came to be used in chocolate milk, toothpaste, mayonnaise, cosmetics and other things. Irish moss became the good green safeguard for the fledgling Catholic colony.

Together, they fashioned or procured long-handled rakes (some fourteen feet in length), brought the seaweed ashore and left it to thoroughly dry on the beaches for days, at which point they packed it up and sent it to Boston to be sold. Boston was a ready market for the product, which was known to be nutritious when made into gelatin—an early health food. In time, it found many other uses as well.

Equipment has changed very little since the early 1800s—nor, for that matter, have techniques improved to any large extent. Specially designed rakes with cast-bronze heads are used. They have twenty-five to thirty-two teeth and a long handle—wooden at first, more likely aluminum of late. Rakers work from small boats called skiffs, either alone or in pairs, each boat having a net to store harvested moss. Mossing can only take place from two hours before low tide to two hours after, as an average, and it is usually done in shallow water, perhaps six to ten feet in depth. Moss is harvested by scraping beneath the plants with the rake. The stems get caught in the rake's teeth, and when the mosser raises the rake, the moss is torn loose from its moorings. When they can no longer rake the plants, the mossers take their haul to a central location to deposit it.

Ward's success brought many other Irish immigrants to Scituate, men and women who knew how to gather the moss, wash it and lay it out on the sands of the beaches of what was called Jericho, which was not at that time crowded with sunbathers. They then packed it in large tubs or bags and sent the moss to market. Ward remained the leader—the chief packer and

Irish mosser. *Scituate Historical Society.*

shipper, the one who found the markets. The industry remained in his family and in the hands of Irish families. They were the only ones doing it, so it provoked no competitive envy from the earlier settlers. Tom Dwyer became the later buyer and processor. Lucien Rousseau was the last to work in the industry late in the twentieth century.

The families of the first two Irish settlers began what would become a colony of Catholics, the first of any size on the South Shore, as well as a prosperous industry in gathering Irish moss. It was hard work, but Irish immigrants coming into this country worked hard at many things, including building roads and railroads. The moss had to be raked from the rocks on Scituate's shores. Then it had to be washed in sea water because fresh water would destroy it. Each day that it dried, the color would change. Beginning as black, it would lighten steadily until it had bleached to white and was ready. Then it was placed in hogsheads and rolled along the tidewater to the place from which it was shipped—usually sheds. There were many of these at one time along the waterfront, used to store the moss until a buyer was ready to take them or have them shipped.

Today, the moss shed at Scituate Marine Park is the only example left. It has been preserved by the Scituate Historical Society with Community Preservation funds. This particular shed has the names of many mossers written on its interior walls. It now stores boats used for recreation. Describing the beauty of the life of a mosser, one anonymous Scituate gentleman told *American Magazine* in 1942, "It's a great farm we have out there. We don't have to plow it or plant it, but it gives us four crops a season."

During many seasons, Scituate brought in 100,000 pounds and was typically the national leader. The moss was sold for a number of uses: to thicken food, to make desserts like ice cream and jelly, to brew beer, to make a Caribbean drink and for medicinal and health benefits. In the summertime, schoolchildren, both boys and girls and teenagers, worked at the tasks from the period following World War II to the demise of the industry, when cheap labor in other countries ended demand for Scituate's seaweed.

Following Scituate's settlement as a Catholic enclave, Quincy and Randolph established parishes in 1848 and 1850. The smaller number in Scituate as well as other towns like Weymouth could travel to these places for baptisms and marriages rather than finding their ways to Boston. Priests would nonetheless come to Scituate to administer the last rites. Miles O'Brien died in 1851, the first Catholic prepared for death in Scituate. He was buried in Quincy. The first Catholic buried in Scituate was John O'Reilly, in 1851, at the Union Cemetery. In Scituate, Daniel Ward, who built the first house on Third Cliff, known as the "Big House," offered it up for the first Catholic mass—two priests came from Boston, Father Sullivan and his assistant, Father Gallagher. Beginning in 1856, mass was offered there four times a year, with Reverend Aaron Roche coming from Randolph and staying two days on each visit.

The first Catholic child born in Scituate was John F. Murphy, son of Patrick and Mary (Kane) Murphy, on August 8, 1852. The first Catholic child baptized in Scituate after the establishment of the Irish colony was Mary Ellen Duffy; she was baptized in 1855 by Father Sullivan of Boston. The first Catholic couple married in Scituate was Patrick Driscoll and Mary Gaynor, on August 30, 1858, by Father Roche at Cornelius Doherty's home.

As time went on, Cornelius Doherty offered his house and barn on Second Cliff in Scituate for mass and Sunday school, although the vestments remained at the "Big House." However, as the number of Catholics increased, no house remained large enough for the community's Catholic services, so a church had to be built. One priest was responsible for many if not most of the churches built in this era on the South Shore. His name was Reverend

St. Mary of the Nativity Church, founded by Irish in Scituate. *Photo by author.*

Hugh P. Smyth, and he was called the "Builder of Churches." Smyth became pastor of Weymouth, with his missions of Hingham, Cohasset and Scituate. At first, under Father Smyth, mass and Sunday school were held in a grocery store—on the second-floor hall of Paley Allen's Grocery Store on Front Street in Scituate.* But it wasn't long before Father Smyth proposed building a church on the cemetery grounds on Meetinghouse Lane. The first mass was held at St. Mary of the Nativity on Christmas in 1872.

Since much of the money for building it came from the mossing industry, it was sometimes called the "Church of the Mossers." Although Scituate now had its own church, it remained a mission for fifty-nine more years. Father Fagan of St. Paul's in Hingham celebrated mass there on alternate weeks starting in 1880. The upper church was then still unfinished, but he continued the work. A successful fair raised funds and allowed them to add pews, lighting and stations, and by 1897, two masses were being said on Sundays. Two chapels were built next, and at last, in 1921, Scituate was made a parish. It included Marshfield and Norwell, and the first pastor was Father Patrick Buckley. He bought a house for a rectory and also built a chapel in Humarock. In the time since, the church has had six pastors and many changes, including replacement of the original church when it was destroyed by fire. The church is St. Mary of the Nativity.

As to the mossing industry that brought the first Irish to Scituate, its influence and that of other historical events is preserved in the Maritime and Mossing Museum on the Driftway, formerly the home of Captain Benjamin James. It has exhibits on such things as ships and shipwrecks, lifesaving activities, Irish mossing, shipbuilding and other nautical effects.

Note: This store was a descendant of the first store in Scituate, as chronicled in an article on the Scituate Historical Society's website. The original store, owned by Ensign Otis, was really a trading post, exchanging, for example, items that came to Boston via the West Indies trade—things like rum, molasses and spices brought to Scituate by packet and of interest to the early settlers. The store was also frequented by American Indians, who exchanged pelts for beads and ribbon. A later owner gave warning of the British raid during the War of 1812, and the building twice served as a post office.

Lighthouses and Shipwrecks

S cituate has a rocky coast with strong waves and currents. Among those rocks are ledges that pose an acute danger to ships when those strong waves and currents drive ships onto them—as they often have. Of course, over a long span of time, the town has had frequent shipwrecks—some of the worst on the Atlantic coast, in fact. It has taken steps to reduce these, and the government has taken action as well, but it's still a dangerous shore. Even the American Indians who lived along the coast and had but a limited knowledge of science were aware of the danger. They feared it and provided an explanation for it.

The town and its coast have a reputation for danger that is well earned. That location on a rocky, ledge-strewn coast makes it friendly to shipbuilding but not to ships. It is a coast that became famous for its lighthouses, for the moss gathered from its rocks by Irish immigrants, for its beaches and boating and most recently—even as recently as 2013—for its valiant fight to withstand ocean storms and the floods that have accompanied them.

Even in the earliest days, sailing vessels faced danger when they neared Hull, Cohasset and Scituate. Shipping and a rocky coast meant shipwrecks. By the early nineteenth century, many lighthouses had been built in the United States, beginning with Boston Light in 1719. Scituate's rocky shoals needed one too. In 1807, citizens of Scituate, recognizing the need for a lighthouse, asked the town to build one. As local governments do even now, the selectmen sought help from the federal government, which was, just then, ready to build one. The government granted the request for $4,000 to build a lighthouse at Cedar Point at the harbor's entrance. Three men from Hingham were chosen to build it, and it was completed in September 1811 at a height of twenty-five feet. It is the stone building that we now call "Old Scituate Light," although it has been renovated in the years since. A light keeper's house was included, the oldest such facility in the country.

The light was meant to protect the shallow harbor, which was sheltered in a pincer formed from Cedar Point on the north and First Cliff on the south. Its depth, and later its sandy buildups, made it hard to enter. But ships approaching it, or just sailing a short distance offshore, faced dangers from rocks, particularly if they were unfamiliar with the waters and the shape of the shore. The greater danger would have been from Minot's Ledge to the north, but the placing of a light there would come later.

There was discussion about what kind of flashing light—red, white, steady—should be used so that it wouldn't be confused with others, like Boston Light, not far distant. The devil, as it often is, was in the details, and this matter required much discussion, so much that the opening was delayed until the following April. A fixed white light was decided on and used.

It didn't take long for legend and lore to drape itself around the light. The most enduring tale was brought on by the keeper and his family. The first keeper was Simeon Bates, who stayed at the station until his death in 1834. Bates and his wife, Rachel, had nine children, including two daughters, Rebecca and Abigail. These two sisters would become heroic figures in the history of American lighthouses. During the War of 1812, British warships frequently raided New England coastal towns. It was early in June 1814 that the HMS *Bulwark* dropped anchor off Scituate Harbor and was spotted by early riser Ensign Otis Jr., who was about to open his store. He gave the alarm. British forces plundered and burned a number of vessels at Scituate. Keeper Bates fired two shots from a small cannon, angering the captain of a British warship as it departed.

Word of the British raid had gone out to other towns, and Cohasset, for one, had raised a militia; when the British came calling, its citizens were ready. At high tide, eleven barges of British soldiers headed ashore to destroy the boats in the harbor and take whatever they could make off with. But they were expected. With Scituate as an example, militia units from Cohasset and neighboring towns had drawn together and were waiting for the British— who changed their minds and went back to their ship.

Less than three months later, Keeper Bates and most of his family were away, leaving twenty-one-year-old Rebecca and her younger sister, Abigail, in charge. The sisters were horrified to see a British warship anchored in the harbor. In a magazine article many years later, Rebecca was quoted in this way:

> *"I'll tell you what I'll do," says I to my sister, "Look here, you take the drum and I'll take the fife." I was fond of military music and could play four tunes on the fife—Yankee Doodle was my masterpiece…"What good'll that do?" says she. "Scare them," says I. "All you've got to do is call the roll. I'll scream the fife and we must keep out of sight; if they see us they'll laugh us to scorn."*

The British thought that the sound of the fife and drum signaled the approach of the Scituate town militia, and they hastily retreated (it was actually the Bates sisters). Thus was born the legend of Scituate's "Lighthouse Army of Two." The Bates sisters lived to be quite elderly. Rebecca later sold affidavits for ten cents apiece, always asserting the truth of her story in spite of doubters. David Ball of the Scituate Historical Society has done extensive research into the story and believes that it is true.

In 1827, a fifteen-foot brick extension and a new lantern were added to the lighthouse. The idea was to make it easier to see. Then a fixed white light was displayed from the lantern, while a red light was shown from the lower windows. Eight lamps and reflectors produced the red light, while seven lamps and reflectors produced the white light. It was supposed to look different from the Boston Light at that point, but it didn't, and ships continued to strike ledges. It showed a red light for a time, but when the light at Minot's Ledge went on for a short time, the one at Scituate Harbor was darkened. After the tower at Minot was destroyed in a storm, the Cedar Point Light was used again until the new lighthouse was built at Minot's Ledge in 1860. It went dark the same night, according to Jeremy D'Entremont, writing about the lighthouse. That may have been an end to the lighthouse's usefulness, and so it seemed for many years. A breakwater was built at the harbor, and then a jetty was built off from that. At the end of the breakwater, a lamp was placed on a pole, and keepers who lived in the old house kept it lit until an automatic one replaced it.

The tower itself was nearly auctioned, but eventually the town gained ownership. Over the years, it fell into disrepair until 1968, when the Scituate Historical Society gained custody of it. The keeper's house is rented, and from that income the property is kept up; today it is a landmark in the town. The light, at this point visible only from land, was relit in 1991, but three years later, the tower was relit and visible to navigators for four miles.

Scituate Light. *Photo by author.*

In an almost ironic twist that seems in a way to taunt the darkness of the light for that long period, the Italian freighter *Etrusco* ran aground at the lighthouse in 1956 during a blizzard and remained there for nine months after the Coast Guard had rescued its crew by breeches buoy. The ship remained at Cedar Point until the following Thanksgiving, when, after some of the rocks had been removed by blasting, the ship was floated off the rocks at high tide. During that period, it had been a major tourist attraction, as crowds of people came to see this strange phenomenon.

It is not known whether the Italian crew, during its short visit to the rocks of Cedar Point, heard the sounds of the ghosts of Rebecca and Abigail Bates on their fife and drum that some say can be heard at Scituate Light. The light is a gathering place on Scituate Heritage Days.

Minot's Ledge (named for George Minot, the owner of a valuable vessel shipwrecked on the ledge) is the site of one of Massachusetts's most famous lighthouses. The ledge, part of the Cohasset Rocks—a reef that extends for two miles in a southwesterly direction off the coast of Cohasset and Scituate, where the lighthouse is located (one mile offshore from Strawberry Point in

North Scituate)—has a history of shipwrecks. The original tower had an unhappy history as well, being destroyed two years after it was built, with two deaths.

The light may be seen for miles, but the ledge on which the lighthouse sits and has sat is almost invisible; the tower seems to rise eerily from the ocean. It had a ghastly history of death and destruction, with no fewer than eighty ships and four hundred lives lost on its reefs by the 1750s. No wonder, then, that the Indian tribe that lived in the area had great fear of the evil spirit Hobomock, the one believed to be responsible for the violent storms that racked the area. It was said that he unleashed them from his kingdom beneath the rocks. The fearful Indians hoped to appease this spirit by venturing out at low tide and offering gifts.

The engineer who designed the 1849 structure didn't want a solid cylinder because he didn't think that it could withstand the terrible storms and winds that often swept over the ledge. Instead, he built one with nine iron pilings that were cemented into the rock below at a depth of five feet. The lantern and dwelling for the keeper would perch on top of those pilings and, he reasoned, be less resistant to wind and water. The first lighthouse was built for $39,000. With this design, a keeper with a sense of vertigo or a fear of heights would have fled at once…and would have been wise to do so.

We have the words of Concord writer Henry David Thoreau, who passed the light that year in a boat and gave us his impressions:

Here was the new iron light-house, then unfinished, in the shape of an egg-shell painted red, and placed high on iron pillars, like the ovum of a sea monster floating on the waves…When I passed it the next summer it was finished and two men lived in it, and a lighthouse keeper said that in a recent gale it had rocked so as to shake the plates off the table. Think of making your bed thus in the crest of a breaker!

Thoreau's perceptions proved to be astute. The keeper's compartment swayed so mightily that his cat jumped off and disappeared in the swirling seas. Three months after he started work, the keeper said that the sea "makes the light reel like a Drunken Man." He quit, and the next one rowed away in the midst of a storm toward Boston, leaving his two assistants, Joseph Wilson and Joseph Antone, behind, white-knuckled, the light unlit. Wilson climbed the ladder to light the lantern and then couldn't get down again. The iron supports snapped one at a time, the light went out, the bell fell silent and the men were thrown into the sea.

Minot's Ledge Lighthouse. *Library of Congress.*

The storm ended at last, and later a fisherman found a bottle with a note in it from the two men, reading, "The beacon cannot last any longer. She is shaking a good three feet each way as I write. God bless you all." One man's body was found at Nantasket Beach, and the other swam to an island, where he died from exposure. The rocks, and the danger they posed, remained. A new lighthouse had to be built. It took two attempts.

A lightship was anchored there until a new lighthouse could be built. But that would be no easy job. The one that would be built from 1855 to 1860 was considered the greatest engineering project up to that time for an American lighthouse. A magnificent 144 feet tall, the tubular structure was made of more than one thousand blocks of Quincy granite dovetailed together for strength and stability. Part of the wonder of this feat was that it was accomplished two and a half miles out to sea. The stones were put together on land and floated out to the shoal, and this was no straightforward task. Once they arrived, the stones were lowered onto a substantial foundation of two-ton stones. But this could only be done at low tide in a calm sea. It was a dangerous task and took five years to complete. Workers were often swept off their feet and into the sea by giant waves. Only workers who could swim were hired, and even at that, a lifeguard stood by.

But all this caution went for naught when a ship named the *New Empire* was dashed to pieces on the rocks, destroying what had been accomplished and requiring a new start. Finally, in August 1860, the lighthouse was finished on Minot's Ledge at a cost of $300,000, one of the most expensive lighthouses ever built. Although huge storms battered the tower, bringing waves that crashed on the top of it, the light burned on, flashing in a pattern of one-four-three, from which it's called the "I love you" light. It can be seen for miles but can only be reached by boat.

In 1971, an automated light powered by solar energy was installed. The previous lens (third-order Fresnel) now sits on Government Island (in Cohasset

Shore Acres
Beach and
Minot's Light.
*Postcard via
Boston Public
Library.*

Harbor) in a replica of the lantern room, along with the fog bell. The keepers' dwelling is there, too, and is listed on the National Register of Historic Places. The island also has a monument to the two keepers who lost their lives in the original lighthouse. It was from there that the granite blocks were assembled (1,079 of them) before being brought to the ledge to build the tower.

Hobomock has gone his way, but he hasn't taken the mystery with him. The light is still haunted by curious things; chief among them is the story of some Portuguese fishermen who reported seeing someone hanging onto a ladder and shouting at them in Portuguese to stay away. Local fishermen have also heard cries for help. After all these years, the lighthouse is still seemingly haunted by the ghosts of the two lost men, who keep the lens clean and warn people away.

The SS *Portland* was lost in a gale named for it in late November 1898, a storm that caused incredible damage on the New England coast and even changed the flow of a river in Scituate. The ship set sail at 7:00 p.m. on the night of November 27, 1898. The captain, Hollis Blanchard of Westbrook, Maine, had heard the forecast for a snowstorm and had been warned by another captain against sailing. However, he did sail on schedule—some say because he didn't want to miss a party for his daughter in Maine, some say because he was an aggressive captain and others say because he believed that he could outrun the storm.

The *Portland* was a side-wheeler steamship, the type that handled well in rivers or in calm water but not so well in the open ocean, especially under storm conditions. The ships were top-heavy and could be hard to steer in heavy seas, but as it started out, there was no snow or rain

SS *Portland. Samuel Ward Stanton, 1895 drawing.*

in Boston and only light winds. It headed northeast toward its regular destination in Portland, Maine, but before it had made much progress, the winds had picked up and become strong—near hurricane force—and rain and snow were driving the steamer back.

Before long, it was reported that the ship had been seen near Thatcher's Island northeast of Boston, but it was not making good progress against the worsening weather. Following that, it was seen three times between 11:00 p.m. and midnight to the southeast of where it had been. It appeared to have been damaged by the storm. Apparently, the captain tried to reach the open sea in order to find better conditions. But at 5:45 a.m., lifesavers on Cape Cod heard what they believed was the whistle of the *Portland*, now far southeast of Boston. It was later seen five to eight miles offshore in a perilous state. There were no further sightings.

The first evidence of the sinking came twenty-four hours after the ship had sailed when a lifesaver on a beach found a lifebelt from the steamer washed ashore. It was followed by dairy cans floating in the surf. Then, within hours, doors and woodwork were found. At 11:00 a.m., high tide brought in a large amount of what was obviously wreckage from a wooden ship. The *Portland* had sunk.

However, the news of the ship's loss was actually sent by telegraph to France and then relayed to New York and then Boston because the telegraph lines between Cape Cod and Boston had been downed in the storm. In all, 191 passengers and crew were lost with the ship, although only 36 bodies were found on the beaches. Many of these had watches that had stopped at 9:15 (it is uncertain whether this was a.m. or p.m.). The bulk of the remains of the ship were found much later on the floor of the ocean about seven miles offshore and have been explored by divers since then. It may have collided with another vessel—perhaps the small schooner *Addie E. Snow*, also lost in the storm, with its remains found less than a quarter mile from those of the *Portland*.

The ships were not the only victims of what became known as the Portland Gale, one of the worst storms to ever hit Scituate and the area. It was felt worse on the South Shore and Cape Cod. It killed more than two hundred people and sank at least 140 ships, including the *Portland*. The storm blew down houses or washed them away from Cape Cod to Maine. Ships were washed up on shores south of Boston. Telegraph lines were brought down, railroads were washed out and many of the scrub trees, pines and other evergreens on the Cape were blown away.

In Scituate, the coastline was permanently changed, as enormous waves cut a new path from the sea to the North River, closing the former mouth of the river and reversing the flow of part of it. The Humarock section was separated from the rest of town and is now only reached by bridge from Marshfield or by boat. Several schemes for creating a new mouth had previously been considered, including the location opened by the storm. In 1829, a petition was sent to Congress for the construction of a canal connecting the river with Scituate's Old Harbor for a cost of $15,000. On April 16, 1851, a storm known as Minot's Gale broke through the area between Third and Fourth Cliffs but not enough to create a new mouth. The warning was never heeded, and during the storm of 1898, four lives were lost and several hunting camps destroyed.

Another Scituate shipwreck involved the pilot schooner *Columbia*. It was coming back from Boston on the afternoon of November 26 during the Portland Gale and was spotted near sunset by the Boston Lightship. It apparently tried to ride out the storm at anchor. But its anchor chains failed, and it was driven onto the shore in Scituate, smashing into a cottage near the shore. It had a crew of five, but only three bodies were recovered. The schooner was badly smashed, a total loss. The *Columbia* that had opened the Northwest had sailed about one hundred years earlier. Now there were two vessels of that name in Scituate history. During the Portland Gale, the lifesaving crew at Port Allerton Life-Saving Station in Hull, led by Captain Joshua James, made many heroic rescues, saving twenty people from six vessels during the storm.

It is said that there have been more wrecks in this stretch than in any section of coast, including even Cape Hatteras. Stories of shipwrecks off the coast include that of the *Cordelia*, a ship built in Scituate that had been on a long voyage to China and was returning when it came to its end on a ledge within sight of its hometown. Then there was the bark called *Professor Koch*. In 1919, its hold was filled with hides and wool from South Africa when it came ashore at Scituate Harbor, another in a long line of shipwrecks off the coast of town. Others probably sank in the fog and darkness or in a storm and could only be marked "missing" by Lloyd's of London, which insured so many of the ships and their cargoes. Only the ocean itself, if it were able, could give us a complete roster of ships that sank in the deep.

Another news-making crash occurred in 1956 when the Italian freighter *Etrusco* was beached near Cedar Point, attracting thousands of sightseers during the many months it was stranded there before being refloated. The list of those shipwrecks we know about would surely include the *Forest Queen*, a 158-foot packet built in Richmond, Maine, that came to its rest on Peggotty Beach on February 28, 1853. The ship had been on the final leg of a 'round-the-world trading mission and was returning to New York City with twelve tons of silver ingots cast in China when it crashed ashore during a storm. The captain, Olney Lovett of Maine, was completing a four-year voyage and had planned to drop forty immigrants in Boston. This was a case where he confused Minot's and Scituate Lights and ran ashore. The forty immigrants were all rescued, but some of the cargo—the silver bars in particular—disappeared. Some believe that the missing cargo was plundered by Irish mosser Daniel Ward, who claimed at the time that he hadn't found anything of remarkable value in the wreckage; however, after the immigrant mosser suddenly had so much money that he could build the largest house in town, doubts began to spread.

There was controversy, then, in the aftermath of the crash, as well as some unfinished business. Over the years, there has been some excavation of the wreck that has brought up many artifacts, some of which are on display at the Maritime and Irish Mossing Museum. A local diver, Tom Mulloy, located the wreck about two decades ago and has been bringing back artifacts ever since. These include two bars of silver, some pieces of chinaware and even an untouched bottle of Worcestershire sauce.

Flooding

The damage done to boats and ships on Scituate's shore are not the only effects associated with the sea and the weather in town. Coastal storm flooding and erosion are also threats to property and even to life, especially close to the shore. As recently as January 2014, scenes of flooded streets and waves dashing over sea walls near the harbor led area newscasts for several days. Residents who were interviewed seemed to have a hardiness that belied the views through the camera lenses. They spoke of earlier storms that had been worse and a willingness to ride it out that seemed to have become part of the waterfront culture. Families who live here in Scituate say that winter weather is the price they pay for sensational summers.

After the January 3, 2014 storm, a longtime local resident, Suzanne Mullarkey, told *Boston Magazine* that living in Scituate is a labor of love requiring a lifetime commitment to dealing with winter storms: "We have been here 30 years, so we know what to do. You do a lot of preparatory work before these storms. Ninety-nine percent of the time it's awesome to live here, but there is that one percent. The main thing is the water comes so fast. If you have a vehicle parked outside that's the really tough thing, because they get totaled."

Flooding from storms, particularly from the Northeast, has been causing damage to Scituate homes near or on the water for many years. Residents don't have to have been there to know the stories from the Portland Gale of 1898, a hurricane-like coastal storm that did tremendous damage not only to vessels but also to homes and even rearranged the real estate at the mouth of the North River so that Humarock became separated from the rest of town; it has remained that way ever since.

There have been many storms since, of course, but one of the most memorable was the Blizzard of '78 (1978), when the ocean rose several feet and inundated homes along the beach—many of them summer cottages that have since been upgraded.

Northeasters also wreaked damage in 1991 and 1992 and within the past few years as well. (The "Perfect Storm" of 1991 brought $100 million in damages.) Each of these storms has also brought more erosion of the barrier beaches (cliffs) and the coastline, a problem that is ongoing and is expected to continue into the future. There are also coastal surges during the winter that cause flood damage and erosion. Homes on the barrier beaches, some raised onto piles after the 1978 storm, are near the edge of the ocean during these unusually high tides.

Scituate has had a high number of claims for flood losses, according to statistics from the Department of Environmental Management (nearly one-fourth of the value of all claims in the state from 1978 to 1998). The town has made efforts to make new construction flood-resistant and elevated at least one foot above minimum base flood evaluation. The closing of flooded streets and damage to property in the recent storm, with its 12.2-foot tides, indicate that this is an ongoing struggle. Sea walls were crested and yards flooded.

Famous People from Scituate

SAMUEL WOODWORTH: THE OLD OAKEN BUCKET

Scituate abounds in marvelous nautical views and picturesque settings, as well as historical buildings, and the Greenbush section seems to have collected a great many of those historic locations within a short radius. The presence of the MBTA terminal since 2007 has led to more traffic and less serenity in the area, but it still has its historical buildings like the Stockbridge Mill. The mill (1640) is the oldest in the United States and is now owned by the Scituate Historical Society. Once a year, it is still used to grind (just to keep it in practice, one might say). There's one of those historical signs on Old Oaken Bucket Road, formerly Pond Street, that reads, "This is the homestead and well made famous by Samuel Woodworth in his poem, 'The Old Oaken Bucket' homestead erected by John Northey about 1675. Poet born in Scituate January 13, 1785." From the road, one can see the old well and a replica of the old oaken bucket. The original has long since rotted away, but the bail of the first bucket was saved in the Museum of the Scituate Historical Society not far to the north.

The poem became famous, regularly recited by schoolchildren over many decades. It was also made into a song that became popular and

Old Oaken Bucket House. *Scituate Historical Society.*

remains the town song for Scituate. The poem has obvious appeal, including a musical-like cadence and pleasant use of language, but its widespread appeal may have more to do with its nod to reminiscence as a valuable function of memory. That it recalls a way of life of Scituate of the Federal period is a bonus. How, then, did this son of a poor farmer with no great wealth of his own and no previous reputation as more than a minor figure in the literary world come up with a poem that rivals "Home, Sweet Home" in its sentimental pull on the heartstrings? One story notes that his wife suggested the poem, but that's uncertain. The lasting things are the poem itself and the bit of history and old-time charm that it has brought to Greenbush and Scituate. Samuel Woodworth, who, as the sign says, was born in Scituate and spent his childhood there, lived from 1784 to 1842 and wrote other poems in addition to "The Old Oaken Bucket," his most famous.

Samuel lost his mother at age fourteen, and his father remarried a Northey, whose ancestors had owned the house in the days of King Philip's War, in which it played a small role. Samuel's father, who hadn't much money, arranged to have him tutored by his minister. The minister saw an inkling of the young man's literary skills but couldn't raise the funds to send him to college, so instead he arranged for him to serve an apprenticeship. The young man thus became a printer, apprenticed to the veteran publisher Major Russell of the *Columbian Sentinel* in Boston, the leading Federalist journal of its day. His stay in Boston seems to have given young Samuel a solid backing. When he had paid for his apprenticeship, he decided, in the footloose manner of a young man unsettled on his future, to move on. He spent a brief time in New Haven and then went on to New York, where he worked for publishers, was friendly with others in the Bohemian circle of that day and eventually married.

The story of the Old Oaken Bucket appears to be about a poet and his poem, but it can also be seen as a poem about human nature—about reminiscences and the hold they can have on us in recalling the past. It is also about the way a single moment in a certain mood can call forth a past that perhaps never existed in quite the way we remember it, excluding, for example, the unpleasant aspects that often are forgotten. So the author of what became a famous poem had been a Scituate man who had not yet succeeded in life but had felt a connection with the literary world—a man who wished to try new ways to make a connection with life but who hadn't found the creative spark to do something really new. Samuel Woodworth, our poet from Scituate, had a lucky moment of inspiration and knew what to do with it.

In one version, he and his literary compadres have repaired to a local watering hole known well to them and where the cognac is supposedly quite good. He is quite thirsty and decides that a drink of cognac is the best choice to relieve his thirst. He has just drained the draft and set down the glass, whereupon he exclaims that it was the finest drink in the world. His companion refutes his contention, exclaiming, "There you are mistaken. Remember the old oaken bucket and the clear cold water of the well."

From whatever depth the companion had drawn this gem of a rejoinder, it hit its intended mark. Samuel, reportedly, burst into tears, left the room and returned to his desk, where the years of his childhood flooded back to him; in a moment of reflection on those childhood years, he set down at once the storied memories of those days in the lines of a poem never to be forgotten—lines that struck resonant chords with so many others of similar childhood memories, now lost but never to be forgotten.

The Old Oaken Bucket House is on the National Register of Historic Places. The house in which Samuel Woodward lived as a youth has only partly been preserved. The valley of which he wrote is the one through which the Herring Brook runs on its way to the North River. It is in a beautiful though changing area. The wide-spreading "pond," the "mill," the "dairy-

Samuel Woodworth. *From The Poetical Works of Samuel Woodworth, vol. 1, by Samuel and Frederick A. Woodworth, 1861.*

house," the "rock where the cataract fell" and even the "old well," if not the original "moss-covered bucket" itself, may still be seen just as the poet described them:

"THE OLD OAKEN BUCKET"
By Samuel Woodworth

How dear to this heart are the scenes of my childhood,
When fond recollection presents them to view!
The orchard, the meadow, the deep-tangled wild-wood,
And every loved spot which my infancy knew!
The wide-spreading pond, and the mill that stood by it,
The bridge, and the rock where the cataract fell,
The cot of my father, the dairy-house nigh it,
And e'en the rude bucket that hung in the well—
The old oaken bucket, the iron-bound bucket,
The moss-covered bucket which hung in the well.

That moss-covered vessel I hailed as a treasure,
For often at noon, when returned from the field,
I found it the source of an exquisite pleasure,
The purest and sweetest that nature can yield.
How ardent I seized it, with hands that were glowing,
And quick to the white-pebbled bottom it fell;
Then soon, with the emblem of truth overflowing,
And dripping with coolness, it rose from the well
The old oaken bucket, the iron-bound bucket,
The moss-covered bucket arose from the well.

How sweet from the green mossy brim to receive it,
As poised on the curb it inclined to my lips!
Not a full blushing goblet could tempt me to leave it,
The brightest that beauty or revelry sips.
And now, far removed from the loved habitation,
The tear of regret will intrusively swell,
As fancy reverts to my father's plantation,
And sighs for the bucket that hangs in the well
The old oaken bucket, the iron-bound bucket,
The moss-covered bucket that hangs in the well!

JAMES CUDWORTH

James Cudworth was one of the most prominent men of Scituate's colonial period, serving in many governmental and military positions and causing a religious/political stir as well. Born, like many of the earliest settlers, in England, he was the son of a minister and of a mother who had been nurse to the son of King James I (and herself a member of a family who had been part of the nobility from at least the twelfth century). James, baptized in 1612, came to Scituate, was made a freeman of Plymouth Colony and joined the church at Scituate the same year. In Plymouth Colony, a man had to be elected a freeman, and only they could vote.

Cudworth used his franchise well and often, serving as deputy to the Plymouth General Court, assistant governor, deputy governor, a commissioner of the New England Confederation and commander of the

Cudworth House. *Photo by author.*

colony's militia. He and Timothy Hatherly were appointed to administer the estate of Myles Standish when he died.

Cudworth and Hatherly had something else in common that got in the way of their political activities. They were not willing to pass judgment on Quakerism, being friendly to the Friends and criticizing the harsh treatment of this sect. Founded in England by George Fox, the Quakers had come to Boston, where some, including Mary Dyer, had been executed. Edward Wanton, then in Boston, was sympathetic to their plight, became one of them and moved in 1659 to Scituate, which had not been as harsh in its treatment of Quakers. Wanton gathered other members of the Society of Friends with him. They met near Greenbush.

Cudworth got into trouble by having Quakers in his home. On March 2, 1657 (or 1658), the General Court noted a petition from "sundry persons from the towne of Scituate" with a complaint against James Cudworth, head of the Scituate military company, for allowing Quakers to frequent his home. His military command was taken away, and he was not allowed to serve as a deputy to represent Scituate, even though he was elected to do so. In 1660, he was disenfranchised in Plymouth Colony as "a manifest opposer of the laws of government" owing to his support of the Quakers.

What had he done? He was accused of rendering assistance to and having congenial relations with Quakers. Moreover, he had put down his thoughts in writing and had sent a letter to England expressing these thoughts. Colonials were always unsettled when a prominent citizen complained to England. Even in those early days, they didn't want prominent citizens complaining to the government in England and getting them involved in colonial affairs. Cudworth's letter had described the harsh punishments—whippings, mutilations and even banishment on pain of death—that were handed out to Quakers.

All was at last forgiven, and Cudworth was once again made a freeman. In 1675, he became a magistrate with the authority to solemnize marriages (ministers did not perform marriages at that time). The same year, he was chosen to lead a military expedition against the Dutch and then against the Indians in King Philip's War. He took that assignment at the advanced age of seventy-nine.

TIMOTHY HATHERLY

Timothy Hatherly was also disenfranchised when he took a firm stand against the oppression of the Quakers and was forced to retire from his governmental positions in 1658. He had served the town and colony well to that point. Known as the "Father of Scituate," Hatherly was one of the merchant adventurers who had helped start the Plymouth Colony; then was one of the first settlers of Scituate, where he was able to get a large land grant; and then acquired large tracts of land in town and bought up more when members of the church, including the minister, left for Barnstable. He bought Reverend Lothrop's house and then sold it to the next minister, Chauncy. Hatherly seemed to be ready whenever Scituate needed him, helping to develop the town, providing for the church and even taking a liberal stand when religious liberties were at stake.

WILLIAM CUSHING

Often called Scituate's most famous citizen, William Cushing (1732–1810) rose to become an original justice of the U.S. Supreme Court, appointed by President George Washington. Prior to that, he had been chief justice of the Supreme Court of Massachusetts, for which he served from 1777 to 1789. Cushing was born in Scituate of a seafaring family from Hingham. His father had been an associate justice of the Superior Court of Judicature, the highest court in the province of Massachusetts while it was still a British colony. He studied law at Harvard College, where he graduated in 1751, becoming a member of the bar in Boston. In 1762, Governor Thomas Hutchinson called on him to replace his own father, who had resigned from the Superior Court bench.

When the American Revolution began, the Provincial Congress dissolved the Superior Court, and William was the only judge retained. Although John Adams was named chief justice, he never held the seat; Cushing was appointed in his stead. In 1783, he sat on a case that involved a slave who claimed his freedom. In his charge to the jury, Cushing stated, "Without resorting to implication in constructing the constitution, slavery is…as effectively abolished as it can be by the granting of rights and privileges wholly incompatible and repugnant to its existence." His statement meant that slavery was incompatible with the state constitution ratified in 1779 and that slavery was therefore abolished in the state.

Cushing made sure that courts remained open during Shays' Rebellion, which protested them, and also presided over the trials of the rebels. In 1788, he served as vice-president of the Massachusetts Convention, which ratified the U.S. Constitution (much of it based on the constitution of Massachusetts).

Justice Cushing was one of George Washington's first choices to sit on the Supreme Court when he became president, and he nominated him on September 24, 1789, with the Senate confirming him two days later. He was the longest-serving of the original appointees and is remembered as having a nationalist view in which he was usually aligned with the views of the Federalist Party (Washington-Adams). It was he who administered the oath of office at Washington's second inauguration.

After the first chief justice, John Jay, resigned from the court in 1795, Washington made a recess appointment of John Rutledge for the rest of the Senate's term, but when the Senate reconvened, it rejected the nomination;

Washington then nominated Cushing, whom the Senate approved. However, Cushing returned the nomination to Washington and declined the honor.

He died in Scituate in 1810 and is buried at the family burying ground at Belle House Neck, now in a state park.

T.W. LAWSON

Most visitors to Scituate appreciate the ocean views. In cases like the earliest settlers, they came from Plymouth Plantation or from England. Or they may have been immigrants like the Irish mossers. Thomas W. Lawson's approach was different, and he, too, was different from most people in town, though he may be one of the most famous. He was never a typical townsman, though.

Tom loved the sea. He especially liked to sail on the sea and was a fervent yachtsman; one day, he would become a famous yachtsman. It was in his yacht that he first noticed Scituate. He had visited many places along the South Shore, and one day he tied up at Cohasset and, from there, did some traveling about. Naturally, he and his wife, Jeannie, visited Scituate, and she loved the ocean views, particularly in North Scituate. The views from Egypt Beach were particularly transfixing, and the couple decided that they'd like to have a place there with those fantastic views.

Tom usually gave Jeannie whatever she wanted, and it was she who chose the location. They bought up many parcels of land and erected many buildings. On a high, undeveloped plain (a "wold"), they would build their country pleasure-palace, a rural estate called Dreamwold. This would not be some cottage. T.W. liked to do things big. In addition to the sea and yachts, he liked dogs and horses, so he built a place to serve as a stock farm. He raised Thoroughbred horses there and had a racetrack on his property, and he raised show dogs, too. Those were unusual things to have on your land in Scituate, but they weren't the only unusual things.

He also had a fire station on the grounds and had telephone communications (rare at the time) running between all of the buildings on the estate; he also had his own electricity and generator, with cables that had been placed below ground. It would become the most famous stock farm in America. In addition to the mile-long racecourse, it had a blacksmith shop for his steeds and many buildings that faced the ocean that were, for a time, open to the public. All of this huge place was surrounded by a white, Kentucky-style

Dreamwold. *Photo by author.*

fence that made it a landmark. In addition to a big house with lots of rooms, Lawson built a small bungalow called "The Nest" for Jeannie and him to use when everything got too busy. There they could remain secluded.

When Scituate needed a post office in its Egypt section, Lawson built it just outside his gates. It just figures that a man like him wouldn't want the hustle and bustle of a twenty-five-mile commute to his office in Boston, so he had a railroad spur put in, with his own train so that he could ride to his office each morning in leisure, in his own railroad car, reading the paper and drinking coffee in private—no struggling through traffic for him.

It wasn't enough that T.W. was a skilled and renowned yachtsman. He wanted to design a yacht that would be like no other. And he didn't want it built at any old shipyard. He chose the Quincy yard of another Thomas W., Thomas Watson, who had gained fame as the co-inventor of the telephone with Alexander Graham Bell. This was the Watson of, "Watson come here. I need you," spoken in a moment of urgency by Bell when he was about to realize that he had made a major breakthrough in the world of telecommunications. There in Boston, Bell and Watson were about to give the world one of their most important inventions. Bell was the idea man; Watson was the one who could make inventions and technological advances happen. He was the one with mechanical skills who could make anything. It was he who put the telephone into the hands of thousands of people around the world. He made millions doing it, and now he was ready for a new challenge. He had opened a shipyard on the Fore River, first in Braintree and later in Quincy. Lawson was about to become a customer. Just as he had at his workshop in Boston, Watson was ready to listen to ideas and turn them into realities.

Lawson's idea was for a new type of schooner, one with seven masts. It would be driven by sail, not engine, and it would have sails on each of its seven masts. Lawson couldn't be bothered with the technical names for these masts. He just called them Monday, Tuesday, Wednesday, Thursday, Friday, Saturday and Sunday—easy to remember. He was less original when he came to naming this new craft. It would be the *T.W. Lawson*, pure and simple.

The boat was actually designed by the well-known B.B. Crowninshield and was the first and only seven-masted schooner ever built. In 1901–2, when it was built, the schooner was the biggest project the huge shipyard had ever handled. Tom Watson was eager to get the contract because the company wasn't making the profits he thought it ought to from its navy contracts, and he wanted a commercial (non-navy) contract to help add some heft to his bottom line as it treaded water through hard times. The *T.W. Lawson* would earn Fore River $240,000, big money at the time. The boat would be 403 feet long and equipped with twenty-five different sails that could be affixed to its seven masts, no matter what day it was. Together the sails could spread 43,000 square feet of canvas. The masts themselves were steel on the lower parts and pine on top and bore traditional though complex names—Lawson didn't bother with them. Wind would be the thing that drove it, and that was strange because we were just leaving the age of sail and entering the age of steam. That is, most people were, but Lawson was his own man, and he was driven by his own ideas.

This wasn't just a boat for recreation like his yachts. It was expected to bring a profit. It would be used to haul freight, and the genius of Lawson was that the space saved by using sail instead of steam would allow for a capacious hold and lots of cargo. He expected it to be a "coaster"—a vessel that carried freight up and down the coast of the United States—not an international trading vessel. Many things that he expected didn't turn out as he hoped, however.

The schooner was launched at Quincy on July 10, 1902, and christened by Helen Watson, daughter of shipyard proprietor Thomas A. Watson. It was the biggest ship the yard had ever made. In fact, as the heavy vessel went down the ways, some people with knowledge of ships were afraid that it was so heavy its weight might carry it right across Fore River, where it would crash into the Weymouth side of the river. This was so real a threat that

T.W. Lawson.

tugboats were readied to intercept it in case that happened. However, they were not needed.

But those people who feared a faulty launch weren't badly wrong. They were just premature. The huge ship was unwieldy and hard to steer. It was extremely hard to turn about, and its deep draft made it difficult to sail in coastal waters, as had been planned. It began to run aground or to list, and it soon gained a reputation as an unlucky boat, which was not good. The company found it hard to keep it manned by skillful seamen. Not only that, but it got no kudos for good looks either. Its seven masts made it look ungainly. Wags said that it looked like a seaborne "picket fence."

The *Lawson* was used at first as intended, to haul coastal freight, mostly coal. But then when the price of coal went down, so did the profits. It was decided that it could carry light fuel oil to Europe, and its fate would be settled, as it happened, in the international trade. It was nearing England on Friday, December 13, 1907, when it foundered on rocks in the Scilly Islands off the southwest channel coast during a ferocious gale. Only two of its crew survived. That was a curious date because Lawson was extremely superstitious as well as reckless.

A Scituate resident, Tom Hall, spent years researching the vessel both here and in England, even diving on the wreck and interviewing relatives of those who were involved in rescue efforts. He has written an excellent book entitled *The T.W. Lawson: The Fate of the World's Only Seven-Masted Schooner*. A *Boston Globe* reviewer opined that the Lawson "emerges as a hubristic period piece, sailing against the tide of history." Those words might also be used to describe its namesake, if anyone had considered it at the time. Sailing against the tide was a Lawson trait, and he, too, may have been a bit of a period piece. Certainly there was no one quite like him. But his schooner is less well remembered than his tower—also an anomaly, now as it was then.

Let's pause here and visit the early life of this uncommon man. He was born in Charlestown, Massachusetts, home of the USS *Constitution* and location of a prominent tower that has become a landmark. Even as a boy, T.W. became known as someone who was bold in his actions. At that age, and even later, he might have been called "reckless." He would take a gamble, and if he lost, he would scramble to his feet and look for the next one.

Although he was self-taught, with little formal education, Lawson learned well from trial and error, and as we have seen, he wasn't afraid to take chances. Often they paid off, or else he figured out what went wrong and turned around and did it right the next time.

By the time he reached the age when he was ready to finish high school, and most of his peers were thinking about a career (or at least a job), Lawson had earned $60,000. And then he lost it. However, by age twenty-one, his net worth was up to $1 million. Early in the twentieth century, he was reportedly worth $60 million. In today's dollars, that made him one of the wealthiest men alive. That was to be his high-water mark, though he didn't yet know it. Lawson was unusually expressive and well versed in literary tradition. He could even write. In fact, he would become a famous writer. But he could do much else, too. The question was whether he could fit all these talents into an already full life. For example, he was skilled in finance, and as the century turned, Lawson was a highly successful stockbroker who had an office at 333 State Street in Boston overlooking the harbor. From its windows, he dreamed panoramic dreams.

A large, mustachioed man, well turned out in expensive three-piece suits and parting his hair in the middle, Lawson was also superstitious. He believed that the numeral "3" was lucky for him and also believed that his huge pocket watch brought him good luck.

Indeed, he often had good luck, or thought he did, but not all the time. One of his Thoroughbreds, Boralona, won all of its races except one. It lost the Kentucky Derby on a day when Lawson wasn't carrying his lucky watch. He gave all the horse's winnings to charity. But he must have had his watch when he and his family and friends visited Monte Carlo. T.W. had such a winning streak that the casino had to close down because the bank ran out of money. So, if the story is true, then Lawson was indeed the "Man Who Broke the Bank at Monte Carlo."

His luck was bad, however, when he had his champion English bulldog shipped by train from New York to Dreamwold. When they opened the box, the dog was dead.

He was good (rather than lucky) at business. He was able to outsmart Standard Oil to control an energy company in the Bay State and then able to collaborate with it in growing Amalgamated Copper, the name under which Standard Oil reorganized the great Anaconda mine. He was clever, too, if not honest. Lawson told his clients to buy the stock, and they did,

Thomas Lawson, businessman. *Scituate Historical Society.*

driving up the price and then driving it down again, with Lawson picking up shares that now sold at low prices. As a broker, Lawson could simply tell clients, "Buy Amalgamated," and they would do it, often people who couldn't afford the loss. One report said that thirty people committed suicide as a result. The enterprise eventually failed, and Lawson took some of the heat from stockholders but became known as the "Copper King."

Lawson wrote a serialized book, *Frenzied Finance*, in which he placed the blame on John D. Rockefeller, who really had no involvement in it at all. When the story first appeared in *Everyone's Magazine*, the first issue sold out in a few days, and future issues were so compelling that the magazine's circulation rose to number one in the country. Not only did it give an insider's exposé of Wall Street's cutthroat practices, but it also said enough about the insurance industry to provoke an investigation.

Lawson enjoyed artwork and nature in equal parts, and his office and home both appeared crammed to crowding with each. Closer examination, however, would have yielded the understanding that here was a logical man with a sense of harmony and that each picture, sculpture and flower fit nicely into sequence with the others. He even paid $30,000 to have a carnation named for his wife. It was called the "Lawson Pink."

If Lawson is remembered for anything in Scituate, however, it would be for his tower. One morning at the beginning of the twentieth century, Jeannie Lawson looked out her back window and saw a steel standpipe that the water company had inserted to tap a water source. It didn't fit with her view of what Dreamwold should be. She hated what this commercial intruder did to her pristine view. Lawson, ever sympathetic to Jeannie's desires, told her not to worry—he would take care of it. Unable to have it removed, he decided to cover it up and got permission to do that.

Now, you or I might have painted it blue like the sky or green like the trees, but not Lawson. That would not have been in keeping with his grand vision of things. Lawson hired an architect right off. And he told him to go to Europe and look around for the best design he could find to cover up the ugly standpipe. The man did as he was told and came back with a design for a *tower* that he had seen on the Rhine River of Germany. It was part of a castle overlooking the Rhine.

From that design, T.W. built Lawson Tower. It's considered the most beautiful water tower in the world. He added a chime with ten bells and a clock, as well as a widow's walk, from which he could look out on the Atlantic and watch his ships carry copper to Boston. That worked both ways: people at sea could also see the tower and use it as a landmark.

Lawson Tower. *Photo by author.*

Lawson Tower is certainly the most photographed and the most expensive water tower in the world. It was completed in 1902 when the chime and clock were added. Lawson Tower was listed as an American Water Landmark in 1974. Two years later, it made the National Historic Register of Places as an individual property.

He also had a flagpole made from the tallest tree ever to leave Oregon. In transshipping it, the conveyance that was carrying it broke through wooden planking on the Fore River Bridge, but they got it to Dreamwold, where Lawson raised huge flags on it.

In the last several years, changes have been made to his vaunted tower. The standpipe began to leak and has been shortened so that it is now only ten feet tall. The tower has been re-shingled and restored. Renovation costs were paid for from mitigation funds paid to the town by the railroad in funding for historic preservation. The bells have been repaired using Community Preservation funds. The town now owns the tower and tank, but it is administered by the Scituate Historical Society.

Besides the book on the schooner, there is one for children called *The Legend of Lawson's Elephants: An Elephantasy*, by Robert Louis Sheehan. It's a blend of historical fact and fancy. Another of Lawson's peculiarities was his love of elephants. He had more than three thousands of them at Dreamwold made of wood, ivory, bronze and even jade. The superstitious owner believed that they were good luck. He also paid for an elephant fountain on the town green, Lawson Common, on land he donated. Of course, the number of elephants was three. A story has it that he hired a man just to count the elephants each day to be sure that none was stolen by any of the visitors. Lawson was fiercely loyal to all of his workers and asked nothing from Scituate while frequently offering gifts. The elephants and the donations gave Lawson a softer look. From his business practices and his writings, an image of a tougher, sometimes even ruthless, person emerges. Another excellent book is *Beauty, Strength, Speed*, by Carol Miles and John Galluzzo, the latter chairman of Special Projects for the Scituate Historical Society. The book has marvelous descriptions and photos of Dreamwold.

Perhaps Lawson's most lasting writing flowed from his interest in yachting. He built a scow, *Independence*, and attempted to enter it into the America's Cup trials, but this was not permitted. The race, run by the New York Yacht Club, had certain rules, and Lawson seems to have flaunted them. He would not join the club or cooperate with it. In any case, his boat was probably not competitive. But they wouldn't even let him try, and that set off his storied temper. Partly in retaliation, he wrote *The Lawson History of the America's Cup*, which yachtsmen have proclaimed as "The Book." Its 3,000 copies were sought after and became collectors' items. Twenty years ago, another 1,500 were printed, and these also draw a good price. But one chapter recounts Lawson's view of his own experiences with the club and gives his highly negative personal views of some of the club members.

In 1906, the superstitious Lawson also wrote a novel, *Friday, the Thirteenth*, which became a movie as well. The main character is a Lawson-like person who tries to justify the stock market panic he caused, but as a way of exposing the corruption on Wall Street. His book harmed him and the stock market too. It was also the beginning of the superstition about the date in the title. Lawson had a lot of bad luck ahead. His wife died, he lost most of his money and he had to sell Dreamwold for back taxes. It later became a restaurant, a function hall and, in 1983, condominiums. They stand yet, along with the white fence that seems to belong in Kentucky. Lawson Tower stands, too.

Ironically, the boat named for him would also sink on Friday the thirteenth. Curiously, Lawson's title may have made the date a symbol of bad luck. A book titled *13* by Nathaniel Lachenmeyer notes that the day and the date were first brought together by Lawson.

When Jeannie died in 1906, Lawson was heartbroken and couldn't function for a long time. He also had to testify before a Congressional hearing about insider trading and didn't do well. After that, he lost his influence and gradually lost most of his money. He began to spend his time in Oregon, where most of his relatives lived. Lawson died, nearly broke, in 1925. His tower remains as a fitting monument to a man who rose to great heights at the turn of the century.

Some historic characters are towers of strength. Others build literal towers and other monuments that seem to recall their stature. But looking up won't tell you everything. For some stories, you have to dig down.

Growth and Development

Like any town on the coast of Massachusetts, Scituate first went through a period of settlement in which the settlers established a form of self-government, made pacts with their neighbors, found ways of making their living that became the basis for future industries and got around by using old Indian trails for roads and the water for most major transportation. Scituate has faced many natural threats over the years, most of them from the sea.

One threat that was different came from beneath the earth, though it, too, originated under the sea. This was the great earthquake of November 18, 1755, which originated off the coast. It was the worst experienced in the Boston area, and its effects were felt hundreds of miles away, but chiefly along the coast. People in Scituate remembered it lasting about fifteen minutes, during which walls were thrown down, chimneys toppled and many houses damaged and nearly destroyed. It happened in the early morning and brought half-awake people into the streets. Residents said that the earth moved in waves like the swellings of the sea and, in several places, broke into fissures that filled with sand and seawater—not only in Scituate but in neighboring Pembroke as well. The rumbling of the earth and the crashing of walls and chimneys was likened to the crash of thunder.

During the colonial period, the people dealt with the tribes; fought against them in King Philip's War, having established an elementary militia; sent troops into battle on the side of the British against the French; and got involved in the dissent that led to the American Revolution. The results of that conflict left America a new country trying to get organized. It didn't have long to get that done before troubles arose once more against Britain and France. These trade wars led to harmful embargo and trade policies and eventually to the War of 1812.

For many towns around Boston, the period of the 1820s and 1830s was one of increasing industrialization. Not so much in Scituate, whose only major activity at the time was shipbuilding, at which its people were very good. But that industry had its limits. Small wooden vessels from small shipyards on a river would find less demand after the Civil War (1861–65). Larger ships, some of them made of iron and steel, were on their way, and the mouth of the North River was too shallow and narrow to handle them. Shipbuilding thus shrank in Scituate and grew in places like Boston.

Land transportation, however, in the form of roads and railroads, became far more widespread, as New England's towns connected to one another with transportation networks. Each town's growth was different from the others, but Scituate's was slower than most, probably because of its location on the coast, away from major roads and, until the end of this period, not connected by rail. It was, you might say, at the end of the line.

The most prosperous period in the town's history came just prior to the American Revolution. At that time, the harbor had thirty fishing vessels at work, shipbuilding on the North River was at its peak and property values exceeded those of Plymouth, as did population. But Scituate's emphasis on shipbuilding and fishing during the early development of the town effectively kept it from developing other industries and the diversity that serves some towns so well. For example, nearby Quincy also had shipbuilding, but it made shoes and glass and quarried granite, along with other small industries. Scituate's commerce was not so diverse. In the middle of the 1800s, then, when shipbuilding demand declined, there was no easy fallback. Agriculture had never provided a solid base; there was still some fishing, though not as much (and there was plenty of competition), and the mossing industry picked up some of the slack at just the right time. There were also small businesses like shoemaking that did well at this time.

During the earlier colonial period, the town had a small amount of industry. A sawmill and a gristmill had been built on Bound Brook and Musquashcut Pond by Mordechai Lincoln (ancestor of Abraham Lincoln), and there had been a tidal mill at the harbor. Mills were also built near Old Oaken Bucket Pond, and bricks were made near Colman Hills. Later, in the first part of the nineteenth century, shoemaking and tanning took place both in Scituate and South Scituate.

One might suppose that the North River would provide power for industries, but it did not. It was a means of transportation into the interior, but its current was not particularly strong, and so it did not become a source of water power. The few dams and mills that were built were constructed along tributaries. These were the usual sawmills and gristmills that are generally part of the history of any town located along rivers and streams, but there were also shingle mills and box mills. Among these, the first dam enabling use of a mill was at First Herring Brook, built in 1650, with others appearing shortly thereafter at Second and Third Herring Brooks and at Chandlers' Pond. The dams blocked the upstream to spawning fish, of course.

Wood from the forests was cut at the sawmills, and bog iron, found in the region, was smelted at Barden's Iron Works, which made 250 tons of anchors every year, including the anchors for "Old Ironsides." It also made cast-iron ploughs, which were in demand for a time. When shoes were made in places like Abington, Whitman and Brockton, tack factories in Scituate supplied them.

The effect of dams on the fisheries was permanent. Even though the General Court (legislature of Massachusetts) passed a law to regulate sluices at mills, the herring and other fish were no longer found upstream. (A sluice would allow passage of river water through a side opening, thus giving fish a way around the blocked main current.) In his 1831 book, Deane wrote, "Formerly, it is said, salmon were taken in this river. Bass had been abundant until within a few year; they are taken chiefly during the winter. Shad and alewives are still taken, but they are gradually diminishing."

By 1890, many swimming holes had been abandoned due to industrial pollution, and a local historian warned that "all the fish would become strangers to the river as bass and salmon already had." Despite the decline in river use and pollution, most types of fish did survive, even if their numbers were fewer. When the Portland Gale of 1898 displaced the mouth of the river, the effect was more profound. The level of tides rose in the salt marshes, and the river became saltier, killing much vegetation along the banks, even the cedars. This flooding put an end to salt haying, and industries along the river declined just as industries everywhere changed from water to steam power.

Pollution reduced wildlife along the river for a while, but toward the end of the nineteenth century, with industrial decline, the river regenerated and became cleaner. Although the forests were thinned, they still remained, and the mills and shipyards did not.

The emphasis on shipbuilding and fishing during the early development of the town had kept it from developing a more diversified

North Scituate, Glades Road and Minot Beach, with a view of the granite outcrops. *Photo by author.*

economic base, and then when shipbuilding began to decline in the mid-nineteenth century, this lack of diversification led to a decline in the town's growth rate. The poor quality of soils also precluded a return to purely agricultural pursuits.

The mossing industry and small shoe shops provided some employment during the late nineteenth century. However, the greatest contribution to the survival of the town was the construction of the Cohasset and Duxbury Railroad, which opened convenient communications with Boston and allowed for tourism and the development of the coastline as a summer resort. This development in Scituate followed a pattern that would be repeated along the Massachusetts Bay shore of Plymouth County—that of very densely developed beach areas with a minimum of public access to the water.

North Scituate and the Glades represented an upper-income component of this type of development. The latter was a private resort, and the former represented the only instance of clustering relatively "high style" late nineteenth-century residential structures in the town. Before this, settlement was located mainly along colonial roads, with the exception of the grid of streets in the area first settled by the "Men of Kent."

The high density of the coastal resort development resulted in a street pattern in which most roads ran parallel to the shore. Much later, the construction of the Southeast Expressway opened the town to suburbanization, and this has resulted in the conversion of a large proportion of the summer residences to year-round occupancy.

Transportation and Suburbanization

Within town, transportation during the late seventeenth through the early nineteenth century was mostly on the water. The town had a series of packets that ran to Boston. These began to run in the middle of the 1600s, and by the early 1800s, they had become regular in their arriving and embarking from a landing on North River at Little Bridge (at the current crossing of Route 3A) into Boston. The first *ferry* across North River came in 1637, and by 1644, there were at least three. The first *bridge* built across the North River was erected in 1656 at Curtis Crossing. The bridge permitted the crossing of the stagecoach from Boston to Plymouth, a much quicker trip than it had been by ferry. Gradually, bridges replaced the ferries at the fording places. These improvements built on one another. When roads were improved, that encouraged the use of wagons and stagecoaches, mostly after the Revolution.

Stagecoach lines offered service between Boston and Sandwich and ran through Scituate and Plymouth. The trip took all day. The stages left Boston early in the morning and reached Plymouth in the late afternoon in time for dinner. By evening, it had reached Sandwich. Several drivers would have been used.

By 1660, locations of all the bridges across the North River had been set, and by the time of the Civil War, most major roads in Scituate were established—roads that allowed people to get around town. The main north–south route was along Country Way, which runs from the Cohasset border southeasterly to the harbor. It later became part of Route 3A, whose original route was far more meandering than it is today. This "highway" ran along roads like Country Way north to South and North Main Streets in Cohasset and East and Summer Streets in Hingham. When Chief Justice Cushing Highway was built in the early 1920s, it ran from the Hingham Harbor Rotary through Cohasset to Scituate, and it still does.

Route 3A remains the major highway through town, cutting as it does from the Cohasset line south through the western part of town to the North River, the boundary with Marshfield. It is a fairly narrow road with many access points, including driveways of commercial areas, except in the southern part, where it runs through the town forest (the "Green Belt"). It connects near its southernmost point with Route 123, the only other state road in town. That road heads west into Norwell. In the other direction, it's a short ride to the commuter station at Greenbush.

Greenbush station is rail transportation, of course, and although it's fairly new in its latest incarnation (2007), the railroad played a big role in an earlier day. The railroad existed on the South Shore, but it didn't run through Scituate until 1871, when the Duxbury and Cohasset Railroad ran through Greenbush. It brought people in, allowed those in town to commute and provided opportunities for commercial interests. A rubber cement factory went into operation on First Herring Brook, and there were facilities at the Greenbush depot for coal, lumber and grain. There were also spring water bottling firms that began to operate during this time.

The railroad not only allowed the people in town to commute to Quincy and Boston, but it also allowed people from outside of town to come to Scituate, particularly summer visitors for whom the seashore was a resort. Development of coastal locations came steadily to the town.

If you look at maps of the town from the eighteenth and nineteenth centuries that show the locations of buildings, you'll see homes spread out along the town's large network of roads, most of them near the road with open spaces such as farms and woods behind them. Land behind main roads was largely undeveloped. At the onset of this period, villages appeared at North Scituate and Scituate Harbor, where shops as well as homes were built.

The major commercial area is at Scituate Harbor, particularly along Front Street, where most of the town's major roads converge. It is also near the causeway that leads to First Cliff and Second Cliff. The area has numerous small shops, many of them specialty stores that sell things like artwork, books, gifts and antiques. One of the larger stores is Welch's, which has been in business since 1879.

Front Street, circa 1920s. *Scituate Historical Society.*

Welch's advertisement. *Scituate Historical Society.*

The Stanley House long stood on Front Street, 1905 postcard. *Scituate Historical Society.*

Dr. Vinal's office stood on Front Street where Rockland Trust is now. *Scituate Historical Society.*

The property where Welch's first stood has been the location of a mill, lumberyard and numerous gift shops and restaurants and was then unoccupied before being restored in 2009 by noted developer Harold Brown, who had worked in Scituate collecting Irish moss during the 1940s and used to tie up his dinghy behind the old Welch Company. Presently, the company is located near its original site and still draws visitors seeking gifts and home furnishings. Front Street is particularly busy during the summer months and maintains the feeling of a small village.

In a geographic or civic sense, the center of town can be viewed as Lawson Park or Green, where there is a memorial, Civil War cannons and (in season) the Elephant Fountain, as well as nearby buildings such as Lawson Tower, Cudmore House, the historical society (which occupies the Little Red Schoolhouse), First Church, the library and two schools. In summer, the Art Festival is held in the area.

Summer has long been an appealing time for the town. While most early development of Scituate was inland, the railroad changed all that. Summer hotels were built along North Scituate Beach for vacationers who came by train. Buses drawn by horses ran from the depot. In addition, businessmen from distant places like Worcester built shingled upscale cottages inland from the hotels and founded what became the Hatherly Country Club, with its golf course.

Boston was now two hours away by train, and as more people discovered the beaches and surf of Scituate, the population doubled by the census of 1910. Small frame cottages for summer use were built up near the shore from Egypt to Cedar Point, some of them for weekly lease and others owned by people who held high municipal positions in Boston, like police and fire captains (especially those with Irish names), helping to establish Scituate as the "Irish Riviera." Mayor James Michael Curley owned a summer home in Scituate with shamrocks in the shutters, like those at his home on Boston's Jamaicaway.

The area of North Scituate and Minot became a substantial summer community built from 1876 to 1898, the year when the area was so damaged by the Portland Gale. The area along Sand Hills at the harbor opened to summer cottages in about 1910, and the areas near the railroad stations at Greenbush and North Scituate became more deeply residential.

During the late nineteenth and early twentieth centuries, the town's shorelines began to become even more developed with vacation homes. Properties near the beach were subdivided into small lots so that many homes

Soldiers and Sailors monument, Lawson Green. *Photo by author.*

School class, 1916. *Scituate Historical Society.*

Sand Hills. *Scituate Historical Society.*

could be built near the beaches. Small cottages were built along Hatherly Road, Sand Hills and Shore Acres, as well as in Humarock. Later, there was upper-class development at the Glades, which became a private resort, and in North Scituate, where high-priced homes were built in a sort of enclave. Apart from these, there were few "mansions," other than the exceptional Lawson estate in Egypt and a few others. Areas like Second Cliff have more recently become enclaves of fine homes.

To the south is Third Cliff, another of the barrier bluffs with fine views. At its southward extension, it looks out on both the ocean and the North River. Just off its coast and in the river is "the Spit," an island/sand bar used by boaters, swimmers and those having parties (which often break up quickly when the high tide washes over it). On the other side of the river, Fourth Cliff and Humarock may be seen.

After the conclusion of the Second World War, when servicemen returned home, they often started families and looked for homes, many of them in the suburbs. Scituate, which would have been out of the question at one time, could now be reached via the train (at least until 1959, when the train stopped). Many people moved there from South Boston, Dorchester and other parts of Boston, and a building boom began along with the baby boom. When the train stopped running on the Old Colony Line in 1959, its place was taken by the Southeast Expressway in 1960, and people commuted by car.

The year-round population in Scituate rose to eleven thousand by that year and would continue to grow. In addition to stand-alone single houses, subdivisions began to be developed in what were once pastures. In addition, summer cottages became winterized and were now permanent homes. The population, which stood at just above four thousand residents, had risen to more than sixteen thousand by the 1970s before leveling off to a moderately rising pace, standing now at about nineteen thousand.

The town is now a commuter suburb, although many of its residents have family or ancestors who lived there or spent summer vacations in town. Now concerned about dwindling open space as well as problems with erosion, drainage and flooding, the town is steering development through zoning changes, with growth occurring around the existing centers and near the stations on the Greenbush Line, which have already brought commercial activity and, of course, a large amount of parking and foot traffic.

Scituate is considered a good place to live and to visit because of its amenities and the preservation of its historical sites but also because of its natural beauty. Scenic areas may be found in many parts of town.

In the southern part of town, along the North River, is Driftway Park, which began as a boat launch from which people also fished. The area has sand dunes, as well as trails along the marshes that border the Herring Brook (which empties into North River). It has a boardwalk and a marsh overlook and is good for walking and fishing. In the same area, there is the Driftway Bikeway, running south from Greenbush and down the old railroad bed to the North River itself. It was planned to run as far as the harbor.

One of Scituate's most popular bathing areas is Peggotty Beach, which has a fairly large beach area and where, even at high tide, people can spread their towels and bask in the sun while taking in the excellent views. It has a large parking area, although not large enough to accommodate an infusion of out-of-towners, who need scarce parking permits to claim a spot. Humarock is an excellent beach, too, and quite large, though even more restrictive as to parking. It's best to rent a place and just dash on over the sand to become a beachcomber.

Apart from beaches, there are seascapes too good to miss if you're able to access them. Some of these are rather restricted, especially as to parking, and of course the barrier beaches and the four cliffs are undergoing erosion.

They still protect the coastline, but each year, coastal tides and wave action wear more away.

On the coast of Massachusetts, the towns of Scituate, Marshfield and Duxbury are threatened the most with storm surges, coastal erosion and the rise in the level of the Atlantic. Of these, Scituate is the most vulnerable.

While not strictly a barrier beach—more of a sentinel of the seashore—Strawberry Point in the north of town (also called "the Glades"). It's not, in a strict sense, open to visitors, but those who can stand atop it will have a scenic moment indeed. You can read about it being "one of the last promontories of unspoiled coastline in Massachusetts." A "promontory" is, as you know, a headland or high point that juts out into the sea, and isn't that a breathtaking thought. Wealthy folks bought up this prospect, but like all oceanfront property, it has its drawbacks, which in this case includes the erosion that attacks such places. However, the granite bedrock that appears as an outcrop is a stabilizing element. Like Monterey on the West Coast, this high point also has trees that have been bent and stunted by the wind, unfiltered off the ocean. They add to the primitive and wild look of the place that nonetheless has that inspirational effect mentioned earlier. It also has granite outcrops.

The property was long owned by the family of Charles F. Adams, grandson of John Adams. It has several buildings on it, but use and development must be restricted due to the sensitivity of its coastal features. They can see what the public cannot—views that start at Cohasset Harbor and Nantasket, with others to the north; Cape Ann and Boston Harbor; and, to the east, the gray, granite and forbidding Minot Light that appears to rise ghost-like from the deep.

Fourth Cliff, too, has great views, and it is obviously prone to erosion. Although fragile, it still provides protection against the flooding of interior areas. Its views, like those of the Glades, have limited access. The cliff is an eroded drumlin that rises more than seventy feet and offers views north to Cedar Point and south to Brant Rock in Marshfield.

To the west, the so-called "Greenbelt" is an area of some length and breadth along Route 3A. It includes land belonging to the Scituate Rod and Gun Club and conservation land that belongs to the town but also some private land that has not been developed. It is ecologically sensitive but also provides relief along the highway from the intrusion of commercial development. It is, however, a likely target of developers, who want to include more tax-paying entities that can also provide services or products

that residents may wish to have. The area has a one-hundred-foot setback on both sides of the highway from the Cohasset line to the North River.

The salt marshes of the North River Estuary are the second-most extensive on Massachusetts Bay—315 acres on the Scituate side alone, along with another 201 acres owned by the North and South River Watershed Association. On the Marshfield side, some is owned by the Massachusetts Audubon Society and is prime territory for ornithologists. The marshes may be viewed from Scituate Conservation Park or from Little's Bridge on 3A, as well as from the Massachusetts Audubon's headquarters.

Also open to the public is Cedar Point and the Old Scituate Lighthouse, with views of the harbor, the ocean and the coastline in both directions. The town had been working on the sea wall there, even up to the time of the January 2014 storm that sent water into the streets. The recently repaired wall was not breached. At the other end of the harbor is Barker's Tavern, built in 1634, the town's oldest building.

One can find scenic places and pleasant vistas throughout the towns, some of them on roads that look rural and are designated "scenic." These include Border Street, Clapp Road, Country Way, First Parish Road, Grove Street, Maple Street, Neal Gate Street, Old Oaken Bucket Road, Stockbridge Road, Summer Street, Tilden Road and Old Driftway. These are often bordered by stone walls and date back as far as 1690. The Driftway was once an Indian trail. It runs from Third Cliff west along the North River marshes to the Stockbridge Grist Mill and Old Oaken Bucket Pond. In the West End is another notable trail, Bates Lane, a historic path through the woods on the land of the Rod and Gun Club out to Route 3A.

The town guards well its historic places and has for many years. An active historical society with many volunteers maintains collections and works on projects that involve Community Preservation funds. These are available in Massachusetts towns that vote to pay required matching funds. But they can be used for things other than historical preservation. Scituate has backed an inordinate number of historical projects, and it shows.

If you drive through town, look for the bright-blue signs that mark the locations of historic sites, of which there are many, including the Little Red Schoolhouse, where the historical society is located.

Opposite, top: The Little Red Schoolhouse, home of the Scituate Historical Society. *Photo by author.*

Opposite, bottom: The light-blue signs point out historical locations. *Photo by author.*

Bibliography

Print Sources

Briggs, L. Vernon. *History of Shipbuilding on North River*. Boston: Coburn, 1899.

Clarke, Ted. *Boston Curiosities: A History of Beantown Barons, Molasses Mayhem, Polemic Patriots and the Fluff in Between*. Charleston, SC: The History Press, 2008.

———. *South of Boston: Tales from the Coastal Communities of Massachusetts Bay*. Charleston, SC: The History Press, 2010.

Daly, Gael. *Humarock from A to Z*. Scituate, MA: Converpage, 2013.

Damon, Daniel E. "History of Scituate and South Scituate." In *History of Plymouth County, Massachusetts*. Edited by D.H. Hurd. Philadelphia: J.W. Lewis, 1884.

Daughters of the American Revolution, Chief Justice Cushing Chapter. *Old Scituate Massachusetts*. Oakland: University of California, 1921.

Deane, Samuel. *History of Scituate*. Boston: James Loring, 1831.

Edwards, Agnes. *The Old Coastal Road*. Boston: Houghton Mifflin, 1920.

Garrett, Edward. *The Pilgrim Shore*. Boston: Little-Brown, 1900.

Reale, Paul. *South Shore Stories III*. Scituate, MA: Peejay, 1994.

Scituate Chamber of Commerce/Scituate Historical Society. *Scituate 1636–1961*. Scituate, MA: self-published, 1961.

Scituate Historical Society. *Images of America: Scituate*. Charleston, SC: Arcadia, 2000.

Torrey, James. "History and Description of Scituate, Mass., 1815." Massachusetts Historical Society Collections, Boston, Massachusetts.

ELECTRONIC SOURCES

Boston.com. "How the South Shore Became the Irish Riviera." http://www.boston.com/news/local/massachusetts/articles/2011/01/09/how_the_south_shore_became_the_irish_riviera.

D'Entremont, Jeremy. "History of Scituate Light, Massachusetts." New England Lighthouses. http://www.newenglandlighthouses.net/scituate-light-history.html.

Irish Central. "The Most Irish Town in America Is Named using U.S. Census Data." http://www.irishcentral.com/news/the-most-irish-town-in-america-is-named-133427563-237789381.html.

Kellscraft. "The Well-Sweep of a Song." http://www.kellscraft.com/RomanceOldNERooftrees/RomanceOldNERooftrees23.html.

Scituate Historical Society. http://scituatehistoricalsociety.org.

Secretary of the Commonwealth of Massachusetts. *MHC Reconnaissance Survey Town Report: Scituate*. http://www.sec.state.ma.us/mhc/mhcpdf/townreports/SE-Mass/sci.pdf.

7News Boston WHDH-TV. "Scituate Dealing with Ice After Major Flooding." http://www.whdh.com/story/24458679/scituate-dealing-with-ice-after-major-flooding.

St. Mary of the Nativity. "Parish History." http://stmaryscituate.org/index.php/about-us/parish-history.

USA Cities Online. "Scituate." http://www.usacitiesonline.com/macountyscituate.htm.

Wicked Local, Boston MA. "First Parish Church: A Story of Scituate History." http://www.wickedlocal.com/scituate/news/x776197310/First-Parish-Church-A-story-of-Scituate-history#ixzz2pj1ELCwQ.

Index

About the Author

Ted Clarke is author of twenty-one books, most of them on history; a longtime chairman of the Weymouth Historical Commission; and a lifetime resident of Greater Boston. He has also written and narrated five television programs on history, one of which won a statewide award.

A teacher for forty-five years, with three master's degrees, he is a husband, father and grandfather and served as president of the Skating Club of Boston and first vice-president of U.S. Figure Skating. He was chairman of the 2001 U.S. Figure Skating Championships in Boston and is a national judge and referee in figure skating, having also written three books on that subject.

He and his wife, Mary, live in Weymouth, a town for which he has written two books, contributed a weekly newspaper article and made numerous televised appearances, including five programs that he wrote and narrated. He has recently written books on Hingham and the South Shore, as well as several on Boston. In 2013, he added to the list books on the Charles River and the North Shore. He does frequent book talks and signings and also appears on radio and TV shows, as well as social media, to talk about history and books.